NON-FICTION

NON-FICTION

*UEA MA
Creative Writing Anthologies
2021*

CONTENTS

ELISA SEGRAVE	Foreword	VII
HELEN SMITH	Introduction	IX
HELEN BACZKOWSKA	Treshnish: The Edges of Extinction	3
JENNA BISHOP	Willow	9
WINIFRED BOLTON	Love Token	15
GORDON CLARK	Moving	21
HANNAH DEE	Broadmoor: 'It's A Good Home, Ain't It?'	27
NINA LESTER FINLEY	Flying North	33
ROBERT GARNER	Extracts from the Diary of an Academic	41
CONSTANCE HARRIS	These Hills of Dark Containment	51
AZADEH HASHEMIAN	Scarf Story	57
LALYA LLOYD	Church Street	63
FRANCES LORD	Gossip as fresh as yesterday	69
YIRU PENG	On Floor Nine	77
HENRY REICHARD	Birth	83
JANNITA SMITH	Fit For What?	89
SHANTELLE STEIN	The Road to Roughton	95
JILL VAUGHAN	The Place of Springs	101
QINGHUA ZHU	Tea or Coffee?	109
	Acknowledgements	115

ELISA SEGRAVE
Foreword

In early 1970, a friend and I travelled round America on Greyhound Buses, collecting underground newspapers. Many US towns had at least one. It was an exciting and turbulent time. In Chicago, before visiting the newspaper office of *The Chicago Seed*, I'd tried unsuccessfully to get into the trial of the Chicago 7 (shown in the recent film written and directed by Aaron Sorkin) and in Los Angeles, one of the underground newspapers we visited sported the creepy headline: 'Manson, Man of the Year'. (Charles Manson and his 'Family' were found guilty of nine murders, including that of pregnant Sharon Tate, Roman Polanski's wife.) We arrived in Santa Barbara to find the bank had been burned down in the night.

Everywhere I went, I wrote down what happened, including many recorded conversations. However, when I submitted this to Faber and Faber (who, much later, did publish my first and second books, *The Diary of a Breast* and *Ten Men*) I was told, disappointingly: 'Turn it into a novel.' Perhaps the editor was thinking – in a more modest way – of Dos Passos's USA trilogy, published successively in 1930, 1932 and 1936, in which Dos Passos used newspaper clippings, biography, autobiography, and fictional realism to create a panorama of America in the first half of the twentieth century. His ambitious avant-garde hybrid books were still called 'novels'.

Today, thank goodness, fiction is no longer considered superior to other forms of writing, and personal memoirs and other types of 'creative non-fiction' are everywhere. Still, nomenclature by authors and their publishers often seems fluid and arbitrary. Some writers insist on calling their very autobiographical works novels; I am not always sure why. One example is Klaus Ove Knausgaard's six volumes *My Struggle* whose obsessive 'truthfulness' he later said he regretted, as it may have caused his second wife's breakdown. It had also enraged certain family members – his uncle was furious at the graphic description of the author's father's death, the deceased also being the uncle's brother. How 'truthful' should writers be? Calling something a novel is not always a disguise.

Rachel Cusk's latest books also have strong autobiographical themes – perhaps they can be described as 'scrupulous self-examination' – and are dubbed 'autofiction'. She too has sometimes received disapproval for disregarding others' feelings though both she and Knausgaard don't shrink from portraying themselves too in an unflattering light.

Certain authors repeat the same material, see-sawing between fiction and non-fiction, perhaps trying to make sense of their own lives. Sybille Bedford's 1956 autobiographical novel *A Legacy*, about her childhood and young adulthood, contained material that was covered again twenty years later in her memoir *Quicksands*, and in 1989, her book *Jigsaw*, described as 'an autobiographical novel', was shortlisted for the Booker Prize. Rather confusing.

Andrew Barrow's *The Tap Dancer* (1992) about his father – in which very little was made up – won both the McKitterick and Hawthornden Prizes and is called a novel, whereas J R Ackerley's 1966 book about *his* father resulted in the annual Ackerley Prize for memoir. What to make of all this?

Surely it must be in the selection and shaping of the raw material that makes a piece of writing successful, whether we call it fiction, non-fiction or creative non-fiction? Just as important as choosing what to include is choosing what to leave out and this can be difficult. In 1979, I was introduced to Diana Holman-Hunt, grand-daughter of the pre-Raphaelite painter and author of the funny and poignant memoir *My Grandmothers and I*, one of my favourite books. I had still not published a book myself and found structure problematic. Diana tried to help, saying that you had to find the right beads to string on the thread. I finally managed this with my first book, but only because I had breast cancer, and had already written my diary of those eight months of my life, from cancer's discovery to the end of the treatment. I am still hopeless at structure.

The pieces in this anthology are never boring, they are all tightly wrought, and none is morbidly introspective. Each one successfully opens an unexpected, different world to the reader and I found this very refreshing. It appears that several pieces, though satisfying in themselves, could also go on to form part of a whole book. I often found myself wanting to know more about a certain character or situation.

Perhaps the main advice we writers can pass on to each other is to never give up. We must keep writing, whether in poetry, fiction, memoir, biography or 'creative non-fiction'. And we must go on reading as much as we can, including each other's work. I have enjoyed reading all the work here.

HELEN SMITH
Introduction

At a time when so many of us have been confined to our homes it is perhaps not surprising that a number of this year's non-fiction writers have struck out to explore the natural world and our relationship with it.

The transformative power of place is at the centre of Frances Lord's *Gossip as fresh as yesterday* in which she relates the experience of her father, the artist David Haughton, when he moved down to West Cornwall in the 1940s. Drawing on her archive of her father's letters, Frances offers us an absorbing glimpse into Haughton's life and work when home became a remote cottage near Nancledra. Moving up the Severn Estuary in *Willow*, Jenna Bishop tenderly charts the importance of these graceful trees to family and the local and economic life of the area in Gloucestershire where she grew up. This idea of being bound to a landscape in an almost instinctive sense (Scottish farmers call it *hefting*) is also explored by Jill Vaughan, who takes us on a walk through the Vale of Pewsey in Wiltshire where the stories of her ancestors are as much part of the terrain as the geological strata beneath her feet. Back in her current home in the Fens, Jill feels uprooted. The old Irish farmer in Constance Harris's *These Hills of Dark Containment* faces a similar fate. Compelling and evocative, there's a twist in the tail of this account of an unsettling house viewing. Deracination features too in Helen Baczkowska's *Treshnish: The Edges of Extinction*, which adroitly weaves together corncrakes, shielings, the Highland Clearances and Scotland's role in the abolition of slavery in a sobering reflection on what Helen describes as 'interlocked pasts'. *Treshnish* ends with an arresting image of sheeps' skulls staring down the path and sheep are also the topic of Henry Reichard's *Birth*, a wonderfully experimental and inventive description of the life of a newborn lamb. It is the life cycle of the mosquito that preoccupies disease ecologist Nina Lester Finley in the excellent and thought-provoking *Flying North* as she travels to the Arctic to try and discover whether the warming climate will enable the spread of mosquito-borne disease. A distinctly more appealing insect, in the form of a beautiful dragonfly brooch, is the focus of *Love Token* by Winifred Bolton.

The Cartier jewel, given by Jacques Cartier to his lover Dolly, (Winifred's husband's aunt) is the catalyst for a fascinating tale of glamour, loss and family secrets.

Mothers feature prominently in the contributions from Azadeh Hashemian and Gordon Clark. In the delightful *Scarf Story*, Azadeh brings a whole new meaning to the notion of not having a hair out of place as the hijab becomes a source of conflict between nine-year-old Azadeh and her mother. *Moving* is a beautifully apt title for Gordon Clark's poignant exploration of his mother's memories, the clarity and colour of which remain untouched by the darkness of dementia. Darkness looms large in Hannah Dee's childhood memories too, in this case the appalling shadow of visits to Broadmoor, 'home' to her uncle, Mikey MacLean. Hannah's powerful and shocking descriptions of the high-security hospital and the ways in which its pernicious influence seeped into her own life linger long in the memory.

The characters that are the focus of the pieces by Lalya Lloyd, Shantelle Stein and Jannita Smith also remain etched on the reader's memory, in an altogether happier sense. Lalya Lloyd gives us bravura sketches of Dick Horsley, her eccentric and flamboyant landlord and her fellow 'PG', Roddy Jones, 'part dirty British coaster, part quinquereme of Nineveh.' There's nothing ordinary about this elegant house and its inhabitants, even down to the dirt on the windows... but I won't spoil the ending. You can't help feeling that Commander Oliver Locker-Lampson, the central character in *The Road to Roughton* by Shantelle Stein, would have been entirely at home in 328 Church Street. As Shantelle explains in this engrossing account of Albert Einstein's journey to North Norfolk in 1933, it wasn't unusual for the dashing Locker-Lampson to bring celebrities to the seaside town of Cromer, but their billet was usually the Commander's opulent cliff-top mansion, rather than the hut on Roughton Heath that awaited the German physicist. The surroundings in which Jannita Smith finds herself in *Fit for What?* could hardly be called exotic either, but such is the appeal of Ido Portal – the guru of 'movement culture' – that adherents travel across the globe to an unassuming Viennese suburb in search of the body beautiful. Jannita's wry and tremendously entertaining tale of her attempt to recapture the physical prowess of her youth also raises some searching questions about the nature of the fitness industry, past and present.

In *Tea or Coffee?* Qinghua Zhu asks 'who owns the past?' as she recounts the story of Shaxi, an historic town in Yunnan, south-west China, renowned as a former trading post for horses and tea. Swiss money 'restores' the site, but at what cost to the community? The resulting incongruities are memorably captured in the image of the traditionally attired local, Zhao, leading a horse 'on which sits a stylishly dressed young woman, wearing heavy make-up and high heels, clearly unfit to walk on these ancient stones.' That fashionista would undoubtedly feel more at home in one of the designer outlets Yiru Peng gazes at from her favourite perch at work – the restroom on the ninth storey. *On Floor Nine* wittily lifts the lid on the lucrative industry that is English language tuition. The reader is simultaneously amused and appalled at the situations Yiru describes in a finely judged piece. Robert Garner is pre-occupied with education too – in his case how to navigate the vicissitudes that accompany his elevation to Head of Department of a Midlands university. *Extracts from the Diary of an Academic* gives us a highly comic insight into the world of contemporary higher education in which metrics rule and management-speak has become the lingua franca.

This diverse anthology comprises the latest work from the 2021 cohort of non-fiction writers studying UEA's renowned Creative Writing MA.

HELEN BACZKOWSKA

Helen Baczkowska's writing frequently focuses on stories of place and draws on her experiences as an ecologist and environmental activist. Helen is currently writing a book about common land in Britain today, exploring both her own and other people's connections with land, wildlife and landscape history.

endcottage92@hotmail.com
www.helenbaczkowska.com

Treshnish: The Edges of Extinction
An extract

> *I'm truly sorry man's dominion,*
> *Has broken nature's social union,*
> *An' justifies that ill opinion,*
> *Which makes thee startle*
>   —Robert Burns, *To a Mouse*

One day of sun, among six of rain. I had wanted a holiday of long walks up breathless hills, or down to quiet coves where seals basked on rocks. Instead, there had been short excursions in waterproofs and afternoons in crowded tea shops, where damp clothes caused condensation on the windows. On this solitary day of blue sky and high, unhurried clouds, two friends and I walked the headland at Treshnish, where a knucklebone of Mull juts into the Atlantic. As we left the road, following a track towards a farmyard, a squat brown bird, smaller than a pheasant, scuttled past:

'Corncrake,' I said to my friends.

They were nonplussed by my insistence that this was a story to tell in a pub full of birdwatchers and that corncrakes are shy, usually only apparent in the rasping 'crake' of their call. I took the sighting as a promise of good things to come.

We followed the track uphill, past white barns and into the 'in-bye' fields. These would once have produced hay for keeping livestock and working horses through winter, when grazing was scarce. Information boards told us the in-bye here was still managed in the traditional way, without chemical weed killers or fertilisers, the fields cut for hay, then grazed through the last days of summer. Wild flowers thrive in this seasonal cycle, which might be as old as the first metal tools that allowed the swift cutting of grass; it is rarely practised on modern farms now, so that meadows like these are as rare as corncrakes. Finding one by chance makes me slowly exhale with relief. I crouched, registering the scent of grass after rain and listing the flowers at my feet: meadow buttercup, tiny white eyebright, several species of orchids that I guessed were greater butterfly, with flowers like trickles of wax and the purples of northern marsh and common spotted. White moths, peppered with black, hung from a few flowers and trailing plants of lady's mantle held last night's raindrops on the frilled edges of grey-green leaves. Lady's bedstraw, with leaves fine as needles, was once used as rennet in cheese making or stuffed into mattresses with straw. It was blessed with gold petals by the angels for being the bedding in the stable when Jesus was born.

My friends walked ahead, shouting they would meet me by the sea and probably muttering about the inconvenience of walking with a naturalist. A loud bee filled the silence they left behind and a 'mew' fell sharp through the sky.

'Not a buzzard,' I thought.

A slipping shape, pale as a gull, stealthily gliding along a stone wall. Hen harrier. I nearly called it out loud. That's another pencilled note in my bird book, recording the sighting of a species that, like the meadows and corncrakes, has been pushed to the brink of survival, clinging on in a few moors and islands.

Through a wooden gate at the end of the in-bye, the land dropped away in disquieting angles of short grass and rock. Millennia ago, a lifting and buckling had left the original cliffs and beach raised metres above the current day sea cliffs and shore. My friends were standing on the broad plateau between the two tiers of rock face, looking out at a scatter of small islands. Joining them, I was aware that only part of me was observing the view. A portion of brain, long since attuned to movement and sound, was scanning the sky for the silhouette of a white-tailed eagle and watching for otters in the kelp on the tideline. Only a seal flipped lazily in the waves and, for a moment, stared back with black, liquid eyes.

At the tip of the headland, above a pebble beach, a narrow path turned inland through a cleft in the cliff. It ended among ruined buildings, so far from the road that I thought at first this must be the remains of a 'shieling'. The word can mean both a settlement in the hills where cattle and sheep grazed in summer and the act of moving to the seasonal pastures. Shieling had been practised for at least a thousand years when it died out in the early twentieth century.[1] First-hand recollections, archived in museums,[2] are often childhood memories of journeys to the hills in early May, with belongings carried in sacks or wickerwork creels while cattle walked

---

1 The Sheiling Project. Retrieved 30/03/21 from www.theshielingproject.org/the-tradition-of-the-shieling.
2 Donald MacDonald, 16/01/20 *Discover Shielding Life in Lewis*, Stornoway Gazette.

ahead, following routes remembered from previous summers. The men remained at the main village, working in the fields, whilst children ran free on the moors and the women milked cows and made cheese for the winter. In the evenings there were stories or singing and beds made from armfuls of heather.

Standing at the rounded stone corner of a house, I realise these are not the summer shelters of shielings, which were often no more than a few poles and thatch. These ruins have the solid, unrendered walls typical of Scottish 'black houses': single storey, a window each side of the door and no chimney, for fires would have been made on the floor, the acrid peat smoke rising up through the roof. The houses are picked bare as bones now, no thatch tied down with twine or old fishing net, anchoring it to rocks against the storms from the sea. I imagine a fishing village, with boats dragged high up the beach and fish in creels carried up the steep path to the houses. Across the moor, I looked for traces of the 'runrig' fields where barley and oats would once have been grown and for the uneven ground left by peat digging, but the ruins kept their stories close. I realised I was seeking a reason for a village between peat and cliff, where even the hardest of work must have meant making barely enough to survive. It was hard to believe in homes and laughter, in thin strands of fiddle music in the evening, or the brazen notes of the pipes; in the warm breath of cattle, waiting for milking in the morning.

I placed my palms on a cornerstone, shaped, or 'dressed', to its purpose and found a slight groove, perhaps where the builder also laid his hand, gaining purchase as the stone was heaved into place. A grunt of satisfaction as it settled. The only memory I divine here is my own. In my twenties I built drystone walls and learnt to choose the right rock for each position: big foundation stones for the base, long 'through-stones' crossing the width of the wall and binding it together. In the evenings of those years, I immersed myself in history books, including John Prebble's *The Highland Clearances*,[3] which recounts how famine, poverty and forced evictions drove Scots into a global diaspora.

Prebble firmly laid the blame for the Clearances on estate owners and clan chiefs, who from 1750 onwards, replaced the meagre returns from farm rents with more lucrative sheep farming. Villages were cleared wholesale, their residents allowed to take only what they could carry, whilst the beams and thatch of the black house roofs were burnt to prevent re-occupation

---

3 John Prebble, *The Highland Clearances* (Secker & Warburg 1963).

and the removal of valuable timber. Clergyman Donald MacLeod, an eye witness to 'the Burnings', wrote of watching 'two hundred and fifty blazing houses. Many of the owners were my relatives and all of whom I personally knew; but whose present condition, whether in or out of the flames, I could not tell.'[4] MacLeod also records the homelessness and starvation that followed the evictions, noting how 'few if any of the families knew where to turn their heads or from whom to get their next meal.'

As life in the Highlands became increasingly untenable, many people sought work in factories and cities, or chanced a passage to America and the promise of a patch of ground in the West. Perhaps it was no coincidence that another book I read, around the same time, was Dee Brown's *Bury My Heart at Wounded Knee*. By piecing together archives and firsthand accounts, Brown allows Native Americans to tell in their own words how, in the late 1800s, they were pushed westwards, then into smaller and smaller reservations. Battles, massacres, and broken treaties finally left them demoralised and defeated as white settlers moved onto their tribal homelands. These two histories, an ocean apart, are connected by place and dispossession, by the loss of familial ties and ancestral lands, by profit and access to resources. They are also kin to a terrible third.

By the late eighteenth century, money from the transatlantic slave trade and from slave-worked plantations of cotton and tobacco flowed back to Scotland. In the early 1800s, sixty-three Highland estates were bought with the modern-day equivalent of £120 million of slavery-derived wealth.[5] This wealth combined with the compensation paid to slave owners after abolition, which today would be worth over £16 billion, to provide capital for Clearances and agricultural change. Less affluent Scots often sought their fortunes by emigrating to work on plantations. Robert Burns was almost one of them, considering a position as a book-keeper on a plantation before finding success with his poetry. I wonder how Scotland's national poet would be viewed now, had he taken that job, even though he could show compassion to a mouse whose nest he turned over with a plough.

Scotland banned the owning of personal slaves over two hundred years before England and many Scots played an active role in the abolition of slavery. Yet, standing on a rectangle of grass that was once a home, these interlocked pasts feel like some of the foundation stones for contemporary

4 Donald MacLeod, retrieved 30/03/21 from www.electricscotland.com.
5 Dr Iain MacKinnon & Dr Andrew Mackillop *Plantation slavery and landownership in the west Highlands and Islands: legacies and lessons, A Discussion Paper*, retrieved 30/03/21 from Communitylandscotland.org.uk.

trade, economics and culture. In Glasgow and Edinburgh, the same history is present in streets that still bear the names of the 'Tobacco Lords' – Buchanan, Glassford and Dundas. And the empty quiet of the glens whispers uneasy stories.

Inside the ruined house, I unfolded a map and found the village marked as Crackaig. Later I discovered that it was not cleared for sheep, but was abandoned in 1830 after typhoid killed most of the inhabitants. The water-borne bacterium, carried in human waste, must have spread easily here, where dark pools over peat stand close to the houses. Local legend says the only survivor hanged himself from the largest tree in the village and lingers on as a shadow sometimes glimpsed in a doorway.

In places, the flooded path back to the road was only passable where stepping stones had been pulled from old walls. My friends and I walked in a small, silent group now. I kept a list of the plants in my head, without stopping to look closely: lurid green carpets of sphagnum moss, white-fluff heads of bog cotton grass, faded yellow stars of bog asphodel. Flurries of the speckled moths lifted from the flowers as we walked, although many of them drifted on the surface of the water. We tried to retrieve a few, laying them on rocks to dry in the sun, but their wings were sodden and useless. Just before the road stood a building, marked on the map as a school, but now converted to a house encircled by a tall fence. On the top of each six-foot post was a sheep skull, resting back on its horns. A dozen pairs of eye sockets facing out towards the path.

JENNA BISHOP

Jenna Bishop worked as a lawyer and researcher for the National Trust and is writing a book about the ninth-century monastery where eight generations of her family have lived and farmed. It is on the flood plain of a powerful river. Each chapter is based on a type of tree.

jennabishop@live.co.uk

Willow
An extract from a chapter

Pollarded willow trees dominate the view across the orchard from the front door of the Priory farmhouse. They are stocky, and often knee-deep in water, with deeply fissured bark and spiky haircuts against a pale winter sky. In summer, their supple young branches and silvery-grey-green leaves wave restlessly in every breeze. Mum used to ask Dad when they were going to be cut back, as she liked to be able to see who was coming down the road. When the autumn work on the farm was done and the days grew short, he would spend a week or so with his chain saw and crackling bonfires, working on each tree in a rotation of six to seven years. Without this pollarding cycle, the branches become brittle and heavy and can split the trunk, or fracture in a strong wind into painfully awkward shapes.

Willows thrive in wet landscapes – indeed, propagate easily from a stick pushed into the ground – and march sturdily through the ponds and along the ditches of the meadows around the farm. Their mesh-like roots stabilise the banks of the waterways, and their long straight limbs are harvested in the winter for fencing and spitting firewood. Here in the orchard, not quite joining in with the apples and pears, damsons and mulberry, they congregate at the edges of two ancient carp pools whose water levels vary with the season and the rainfall, now that their clay linings have collapsed. The pools sometimes reveal the leat between them by joining together at flood time. As children, we rushed out to launch Daisy, the tubby little rowing boat, and try out this exciting new navigation. It has always been of sadness to Dad that permission could not be obtained to excavate and restore these watery larders of the old abbey. And so they are half themselves, filling and emptying to the rhythms of the river.

Straight and easy to bend, the branches of the white willow (*Salix alba*) have many uses on a farm. The long straight poles and thicker stakes make 'good cheap poles', Dad says, and the pliable young shoots, called rods, can be used in the weaving of hurdles and baskets. Up to the middle of the 20th century, there was a thriving basket-making industry in the parish. Young trees used for basketry were known locally as *withies* or *osiers* and were grown beside the river, on the lane down to Odda's Chapel, and behind the school. There are places in the village still known as the *withy beds*.

Willow grows extremely quickly. In one season, from late May to early October, a single rod can reach up to eight feet long. Traditionally, new beds were planted in the spring using sticks from the previous winter's harvest, and the last year's fallen leaves provided nutrition in the wet soil. The bed would not be fully productive in its first three years, but once it was well established, with careful management, could last up to thirty years. The rods were soaked and stripped of bark (women and children's work) to reveal the smooth, white, flexible wood.

In the nineteenth century, as a result of the Industrial Revolution, demand for basket-ware products increased steeply, and from the mid-1800s the production of *kipes* or *kypes* for the carrying of coal and other industrial uses became a significant source of income for families in the village.

Many of the harvested withy rods were bundled and sent down the river to larger manufacturers of baskets down on the Somerset Levels; but several basket-makers worked locally, with their finished baskets taken by tug to be sold at the Docks in Gloucester, or in the coal-mining areas of the Forest of Dean. In the farmhouse, kipes were used for firewood in the sitting rooms of both my parents and grandparents. It was my job to lug them over to the log shed for filling up.

The basket-makers also made *putcheons* or *putchers* for the fishing of salmon and eels. These long cylindrical basket traps, similar to those used in the Fens, were cleverly woven, with one or two constricted throats or *chale* valves inside, directing a fish towards the narrow end so that, once caught, it was unable to turn around and get out. The traps were baited with a piece of rabbit or lamprey in the narrow end of the basket and the opening was stopped with a wooden plug. It was weighted with stone, laid in the river and tethered to the bank. A hand-coloured 1738 map of the parish, prepared for the landlord, Lord Coventry, shows a little fishing boat using one of these baskets.

In addition, elver nets like giant ladles were constructed from long poles and muslin. On March and April nights, millions of writhing young eels or *elvers*, the length of my finger, made their way up the river, having drifted as larvae for three years since their birth in the Sargasso Sea. Elvers are less plentiful now. It is not clear whether this is from over-fishing, changes in the river or climate, or other environmental impacts across the Atlantic, but the few caught are sold live at extremely high prices. The trade has become competitive. Smuggling is rife, and there have been violent quarrels on the riverbank. Local people scarcely see elvers now, but I remember Harry Pope, a tall gentle man like Roald Dahl's BFG who had been the farm's cowman, arriving each year with a tin pail full to the brim.

Dad tells me that Harry would sometimes be up all night on the river fishing for elvers from his punt, and then be ready, with his sleeves rolled up, to milk the cows at dawn the next day. One morning when he had finished, he asked if he could borrow a tractor and trailer for a few hours. He and his brother had caught more than a ton of elvers overnight and needed to transport them from the riverbank. In those days, elvers were so prolific that villagers used to let them die and dry out and then use them to fertilise their vegetable plots.

In the light from the stable door of the kitchen, the surface of the bucket on the doorstep glittered and slid with transparent glassy wriggles. We danced around it, daring each other to stick our hand in – trembling with horror, and yet finding the little things magnetically endearing. 'Not dealing with those!' Mum would say when the gossiping was done and the door was closed, but we all knew she would. Beating up a couple of eggs, and heating a large frying pan, into which she chopped small pieces of bacon, she cooked the elvers alive, and offered up a plate of yellowy-grey, opaque shoelaces for us to enjoy. I thought they were very rubbery. Dad winked and twinkled as he told us that in pubs up and down the river, men were competing to eat whole pints of elvers. We thought he meant alive, swimming in beer. 'How would you fancy that?!'

After he retired, Harry's punt was still tied up to a big willow tree near his family's long-gone cottage on the riverbank. The roots of this tree arched out over the water like flying buttresses, and Granny would take me there to fish.

I perched out over the brown water, wielding a primitive rod cut from the tree. I had run my cupped hand down the length of the stick to strip it of its alternately placed leaves. Between the nodes, the bark was smooth and reddish-green. I then tied an oversized hook on to a length of too-thick string and attached it to the end. With my penknife, I had scoured a ring around the circumference of the stick for the twine to sit in, so that it wouldn't slip off when I dangled my worm down into the current. The band where I had removed the bark was white and moist and smelt of cucumbers. That morning, I had dug earthworms with Grandpa in the kitchen garden, and they were kept ready in one of his green and gold Wills 'Golden Virginia' pipe tobacco tins. I don't remember ever catching a fish.

A version of that tree is still there. An old willow can split and regenerate from its broken parts, becoming contorted and semi-horizontal, with shattered boughs protruding at difficult angles and new straight limbs forming from jagged stumps. This stretch of the Severn is not deep, and the water laps in the rust-coloured sand at the tree's feet for most of the year. When the floods rise, though, it passes with some force through the higher branches. There is often a levelled line of dirty dried grass and debris hanging in strands where it has been left by a receding flood. But each spring, the creamy pollen-tipped flowers, the *pussies* of the pussy willow, fluff up ready for Easter displays, and the long, pointed leaves break out again – fresh green on one side, downy and silvered underneath. Later, eager pioneering seeds will launch off in the wind and the water.

In *A Book of the Severn*, published in 1920, the local historian A G Bradley takes a walk along this stretch of the river:

As it swishes moodily along over its reddish, sandy bottom, so wide and shallow in places, one can understand how it was that there were fords here, before the days of locks and dams.

A thousand years ago there was a sandy island here, where King Cnut and Edmund Ironside met to divide up the kingdoms of England. This part of the Severn has always wanted to meander and be shallow and slow. Navigation was difficult at times and, over the years, the riverbed has been repeatedly dredged to make it less hazardous. In 1846, one of my great-great-great-grandfathers, then a young man of twenty-two, was working as the superintendent of a team of dredgers on the river between Worcester and Gloucester. He kept a diary of his work up and down the waterway – of account-keeping, completed lengths, and drunken squabbles between the *navvies*.

In those days, the river was busy with large barges. Heavy loads of coal chugged up the navigation from the Forest of Dean to the manufacturing industries of the West Midlands. Later, petrol and diesel were transported up the Severn until well after the Second World War. On a different scale, horse-drawn barges or *trows* were loaded with baskets, hay, and fruit at riverside inns up and down the river – the Yew Tree at Chaceley Stock and the White Lion, known to us as the Coal Hole. Hay from local farms was built into ricks on the boats before being tied down and towed on up to feed the working horses of Wolverhampton. Fruit baskets were taken up the Avon to the extensive orchards in the Vale of Evesham, and wheat to Healing's Mill at Tewkesbury for milling into flour. The movement of all these vessels up and down the river churned up its bed and silt gathered at different points, according to the amount of rainfall and the direction of the wind.

The construction of a navigation weir near Gloucester, nine miles south of the village, in the 1870s, also affected the flow of the river, and the reach of the Severn Bore. The Bore is a forceful tidal wave caused when incoming waters from the Bristol Channel meet a narrowing of the river just below Gloucester. This constriction creates a sizeable wave that people ride for several miles on surfboards, and in canoes and small craft. Before the building of the weir, it used to reach Tewkesbury at its spring and autumn peaks, but I have only seen a very tame turning of the tide here – a small wave of a few inches, pulling a sheet of choppy ripples and fallen willow leaves over the water's surface.

WINIFRED BOLTON

Winifred Bolton is a former NHS Consultant Clinical Psychologist, specialising in Borderline Personality Disorder. She headed a service in central London. After leaving the NHS, instead of private practice, she decided to write, exploring her interest in the two-way relationship between external and internal reality.

winifredbolton@btinternet.com

Love Token
An extract

It's a jewelled dragonfly brooch. Tiny, not like Lady Hale's[1] fierce insects which draw attention to themselves. My brooch doesn't shout 'look at me!' Instead, on the rare occasions when I wear it, it nestles gently on my collarbone, waiting to be noticed. It has a pear-shaped body of ruby, and a yellow diamond head. The eyes are colourless little diamonds, like minuscule drops of water. The largest stones make up the wings, citrine on the upper side, sapphire on the lower side. The tail consists of two small emeralds and three clear diamonds. It's all set on a bar of rose-cut diamonds terminating in circular sapphires. Our local jeweller guesses it's French and dates from around 1920. He's right about the former, and almost right about the latter. I know because its original owner, my husband's aunt, Dorothy (Dolly) White, who was born in 1899, received it as a gift when a young woman from her lover, Jacques Cartier.

[1] Former President of the UK Supreme Court.

A piece of jewellery can be precious for its beauty, the value it can command in the marketplace, and for what it means. The dragonfly brooch is protected by a soft pouch in my jewellery box and means a lot to me. Along with two Cartier necklaces, also gifts from Jacques, the brooch came to me on the death of my mother-in-law. She inherited them from Dolly. I intend, when the time is right, to give them to my daughter. At the moment, she has no interest in either vintage jewellery or family history. She prefers cheap jewellery which she can lose without incurring anybody's wrath.

My mother-in-law, Norma, was very beautiful when she was young. In the style of Elizabeth Taylor: dark, lustrous, wavy hair, black arched eyebrows, voluptuous lips. My boyfriend, Simon, hadn't mentioned it. I was told about her beauty by Gordon, my soon to be father-in-law, the first weekend I visited and was duly shown the photos and home movies. In her eyes, she had also been professionally successful. She had achieved, from inauspicious beginnings, the position of headmistress of the American School in Singapore. Her mother had died when she was aged three from an asthma attack. She and her sister, Margaret, were cared for by relatives in Belfast until their father remarried and produced four more daughters. Margaret also died from an asthma attack during her honeymoon, when she was twenty-two. Norma suffered from asthma herself, terrifyingly, all her adult life.

She and Gordon made a glamorous pair. A photograph from the late 1950s shows them at Raffles Hotel in Singapore, seated at a table with four other couples. They are the most attractive. Their self-projection was calculated and not just in photos. After post-war Britain, they relished the colonial lifestyle of cheaply obtainable servants, sports cars and socialising most evenings. Their daughter spoke mainly Cantonese until she went to school.

This extracted a price from the children, who didn't feel at the forefront of their parents' consciousness. In many ways, I was the daughter Norma had wanted, academically high achieving, attentive to appearances. But my successes were also a source of rivalry. She picked fights with me when she'd had too much to drink. Never Simon, always me, and sometimes Gordon. Mostly, I tried not to respond. But on one occasion when she was boasting that she had never been subject to sexual discrimination, I could not hold back. She seemed to believe that beauty conferred immunity to discrimination.

'Norma, you worked most of your adult life for the British Colonial Government, and you have no pension as a married woman. That's sexual discrimination.'

She took this as a statement that her career had been a failure.

The extent of the distance travelled though was evident when, on the day she died from pneumonia at age eighty-five, it was me she wanted next to her for reassurance, more than her son. Leaving me the Cartier brooch told me that she loved me.

Soon after the brooch came into my possession, I took it to Cartier on New Bond Street for valuation. I told the French Cartier jeweller, Denis was his name, the story of Dolly and Jacques Cartier. He examined the brooch intently with his magnifying loupe and confirmed that the quality and style of the workmanship was indeed Cartier. In response to the love affair between a young woman and a married man, her employer and fifteen years her senior, he said 'naughty boy' in a French accent that cannot be reproduced on paper. He also told me that it was clear from the beauty of the stones, particularly on the underside where they are less easily seen, that the brooch was a one-off, commissioned directly from the workshop as a personal gift, not for commercial sale.

I'm looking at a photograph of Jacques Cartier. I bought it online from a portrait gallery. He's sitting behind a large embossed and carved desk in what must have been his office in the New Bond Street showroom. The desk is placed in front of a mirror, so you can see the back of his beautifully shaped head. He's looking straight into the camera, unsmiling, his slicked-back black hair and elongated moustache reminiscent of an earlier version of Lord Lucan. He's smartly dressed in a three-piece pinstripe suit. But the most striking feature of his clothes are the shoes adorning his feet, which are carefully crossed at the ankle. They are two-tone spats, with three buttons at the side, usually worn outdoors. The shoes look incongruous in this elegant room, amidst the Persian rugs, the taffeta curtains, the candle shaped sconces, and Chinese vases. I think the shoes speak of a chink in that otherwise magnificent armoury.

The need to earn may not have been the main driver, but Dolly had gone to work as a pearl matcher at Cartier, London, sometime around 1920. Pearl matching might sound like a lowly, repetitive occupation, but it required a high degree of skill. No two pearls are ever exactly the same, so they have to be sorted by size, shape, colour and lustre. Then the matcher has to identify enough pearls that are sufficiently similar to make up a necklace. Even for a highly trained and experienced expert, this can involve trawling through more than 10,000 pearls.[2]

By the time she began work at Cartier, Dolly was living with her father and stepmother, George and Amy, and stepbrother, John, at Maycliffe, a large Edwardian villa in Flower Lane, Mill Hill, London. In the early part of the century, it was as rural as its name suggests. A long curving drive, flanked by lawn and autumn flowering bulbs, formed an imposing approach. George and Amy's son, Gordon, was born in 1921. Gordon was to become my father-in-law many years later.

Through Amy's family, Dolly acquired a large number of step-cousins, some of whom were of a similar age to her, and they frequently gathered at Maycliffe to eat, play tennis, cycle in the countryside and gossip. A recurring image in photos shows her posing, behind the carved parapet at the front of the house, with a fair-haired, besuited man. She is looking straight into the camera, as if to challenge the photographer's presumptuous take on the relationship. This was one of her suitors, Harold, a South African businessman, keen for her hand in marriage. She does not look relaxed in his company and did not marry him.

George White, Dolly's father, was tall, easily a head above his peers, and good looking. He had trained as an accountant and was inhabiting successively grander homes. He became a Freeman of the City of London and was treasurer of his Masonic Lodge. But he had a secret. His first wife, Theresa, was no longer living with him by 1901, leaving him with two small daughters, Mabel and Dolly. Theresa's disappearance was shrouded in mystery by the family, as if it were associated with something shameful, like mental illness or suicide. George's sister, Lucy, took on the role of housekeeper and mother for Dolly and Mabel, until he married Amy Larondie in 1921. This proved to be an eventful year for him: marriage to Amy, birth of his son Gordon (my father-in-law), and the death of his daughter, Mabel. In order to hide the existence of the first marriage, Dolly was presented to Amy as George's sister, not his daughter, despite being twenty-four years his junior. Gordon believed Dolly was his aunt, not his half-sister until 1963, when he was aged forty-two.

George's company, Moss Isaacs Ltd. of 122 Cannon Street, London EC4, had manufactured small scale munitions under government contract during World War One. By the time Dolly was working at Cartier in the 1920s, George's fortunes were on the wane. It took some years for the edifice to crumble; meanwhile the family continued to live in some style, with good

2   www.american.pearl.com accessed December 15, 2020.

quality clothes, servants and seaside holidays. Come 1935, George had lost everything. George's business partner, Moss Isaacs, committed suicide. Amy and George downsized houses several times until they pitched up in Worthing to run a boarding house.

Despite the loss of the family lifestyle, Gordon was able to continue his education at Haberdasher's Aske's School, paid for by the Freemasons, until he joined the RAF in 1939. After the war he went up to Oxford to study Politics, Philosophy and Economics. His son (my husband) followed him there in due course. The loss of status imbued Gordon with a lasting sense of being déclassé. The need for a beautiful wife may have stemmed from this. We call it 'arm candy' these days, a trophy wife to support the ailing ego of a wounded man.

Dolly was less wounded by George's reversal. It wasn't much more than a return to the conditions of her early childhood. But she was now an adult, and able to earn her own living at Cartier. Then in 1937, Jacques Cartier bought her a modest suburban bungalow in Northwood Hills, London. By this time, Jacques and Dolly's relationship had settled into one between supportive employer and employee, but it seems that Jacques still felt a personal obligation to her. He left Britain for France at the outbreak of war and died from a respiratory illness in 1941. George lived with Dolly in Northwood Hills until he died in 1972 aged ninety-seven. Dolly did not marry or have children. She worked at Cartier until her retirement.

The Cartier jewellery passed from Dolly to Norma to me. There were parallels between her life and Norma's. Both suffered the loss of their mother at a very early age, and the death of a beloved older sister at the cusp of adulthood. They shared the imposition of a stepmother and associated step and half-siblings. I did not lose my mother until she was ninety-seven, but I lost my sister, emotionally if not physically, when she was brain damaged in a road traffic accident when I was nineteen. Dolly and Norma forged a career at a time when it was more difficult for women to do so. It's not surprising that they chose to express their female identity in the domain of work where they had more control, rather than the hit-and-miss of motherhood. Norma found a husband who engaged with her in a folie à deux of narcissism, which may have protected her from the inner emptiness incurred as a result of early deprivation, but was then revisited on her children. Dolly was caught between a glamorous French jeweller and a Victorian father who passed her off as his sister for his own ends, and when abandoned by his wife, permitted her to look after him until the day he died.

GORDON CLARK

Gordon Clark is an actuary with a passion for the stories that bring family histories to life. Understanding our ancestors' lives and times reconnects us with those who made us, and helps us understand who we are. Walking in their footsteps connects us to the landscape of our shared past.

gordon.clark1145@gmail.com

Moving

Did I tell you they moved my bed again last night? It's the one complaint I have about this place. That and the problems we have with everyone's things going missing all of the time. And also there's no one to talk to. Half the people in here don't even know what day of the week it is, let alone want to have a decent conversation, so I'm glad you've come to see me.

Have you heard any more about my mother and father? I haven't heard anything about them since it happened. I was talking to Dad the other night. He was sitting in the kitchen, where he used to sit. They've done it all up. It's all modern now, with those shiny cupboards and rails, but I still recognise it, just as it was when I was growing up. My room was up in the attic, and we had gas mantles on each set of stairs, and I used to have to take a candle with me when I went up to bed, and they made such frightening shadows that I had to have someone come up the stairs with me. Dad was reading stories to me in bed. He never told me fairy stories because I didn't like all that nonsense, but he used to tell me about when he was a boy, with his sisters having to drag him to school and all the children going around without shoes.

Have a look in that drawer there. I think there's a folder of photographs and things my son printed out… Try in the bottom of the wardrobe. As I say, things keep getting lost. Oh, that's it, you've got them. Someone must have put them in the bedside cabinet. Yes, that's me there, on the beach with my sisters. They were much older than me. Mum would take in lodgers in the summer in order to pay the rates. I remember one of them was called Oliver Sutton and we girls all used to call him All-of-a-Sudden and thought it was very funny. When the lodgers came I had to move out of my bedroom and I had to sleep on a camp bed downstairs. We used to have to go and fetch a block of ice from the fishmonger's before school. There were no refrigerators in those days.

Didn't someone ask if we wanted a cup of tea? They've been a long time, haven't they? I expect they've forgotten about you. Perhaps we should go and find someone. But I expect they're all busy.

Oh yes. Those. Those are some of my school reports. Look at those marks. Second in the class… a most excellent worker and shows great intelligence. Yes, well, that was before the war came. That's when all the fun and games started, didn't they? I was only just ten when I remember Mum coming up to my bedroom and telling me I was going to be evacuated. Of course I didn't know what that meant. I don't remember the preparations, but I do know that Dad made me a canvas haversack and that he stamped my initials on a spoon and fork. We went by coach to the station and then on a train up to Staffordshire. I'd never been anywhere before without my parents. I remember how awful it was sitting in that large village hall waiting to be chosen. We were almost the last to be chosen and then a large lady said she'd take Olive and me. Well I'd never liked Olive, so I don't know why she did that. I remember the cottage as if it was only yesterday. We sat on a large, high-backed, wooden settle with no cushions and had gooseberry pie. We were so nervous that we got the giggles. Olive and I had to share a double bed upstairs. There was no bathroom, just a toilet at the bottom of the garden, and so we had potties under the bed.

Ah, the tea at last. Thank you, dear. You can put it down on the side there and we'll help ourselves. Have you found my bag with all my pens and paper in yet? I know I put it down by my chair, but someone must have moved it.

Oh yes, that one's of me as the carnival princess. I remember we all had to audition in the school hall, walking round to music. I never got to take part in the procession though, because Mum and Dad had moved to Sheffield and Mum managed to get me home again, so by the time I was eleven I had moved again, to Sheffield. We rented some rooms a mile or so from the city centre. There were only two bedrooms and so my bed was in a little alcove, like a cupboard under the stairs with a little curtain over the front. I passed the eleven-plus, but I ended up having to go to the Grammar School in Ramsgate when Mum and Dad moved back down to Kent.

This tea's only just about lukewarm. Now that's something, isn't it, you'd think these girls here would know how to make a decent cup of tea. Wouldn't it be nice to get out of here and go and have a nice cup of hot tea. Ah, that's a good one of my dad. I loved my dear old dad you know. With three daughters, I was the son he never had. He taught me a lot you know. We used to do woodwork together. I remember I made a box for my sister with a wiggly back so she could use it for her curlers.

We were always round at the aunts' house because it was just across the square and Mum used to meet me after school. I used to have to sit on a little stool and read a book because little girls were to be seen and not heard and mustn't listen to grown-ups' conversations. My grandad used to live with the aunts you know, but they made sure he stayed out of sight. He cleared out people's junk and I don't think he ever made any money out of it, but he always found something for me to take home. He used to pick up all the old cigarette ends and spend the evening extracting the tobacco for his pipe. I think the aunts were quite ashamed of him and he lived downstairs with his bed in the kitchen and a rocking chair. He always dressed in black and wore a black Homburg hat and his coat was long and had big pockets. I remember he always had sweets in the pockets – sometimes it was chocolate, which was dusty looking as it was made in large blocks and chopped up in the shops. But then on Sunday he used to dress up with a white silk scarf and travel for miles preaching at the local chapels. At Christmas we stayed the night at the aunts', in a big bedroom that overlooked the Square and I remember Christ Church's clock striking the hours all night.

Did I tell you I went to see Aunt Alys last week? I went all by myself. They were just sitting down to tea and she said there was no room for me at the table, and she got very fierce, so I had to sit on my own and then I think they forgot about me. Can you believe it? In the end I just had to get up and come back.

No, I don't bother with the TV now. I can't get the blessed thing to work and there's nothing on it anyway. If they find my bag with the pens and paper I've been writing a letter to my friend Vera asking if she can come and fetch me. But I don't know how I'm ever going to be able to get it to her when they won't let me out of here. I do hope the girls will find my bag. They have a real problem here with things going missing.

Did I tell you about the problems they are having here with things going missing? The girls do their best but they keep moving the beds around so no one knows which is their room and all the things keep going missing. Look in the wardrobe; those aren't my clothes. It really does upset me. I've got nothing to wear here except this blessed old cardigan and these old pyjamas. Well, yes, it may have my name on the label, but it isn't mine. I wouldn't have a blouse like that.

Yes, you can take the tea things. No, I don't know. What was the choice again? Sausages and mash, or chicken and beans, well it doesn't really matter to me, it all tastes the same to me here, and it's never hot.

You should see the table manners of some of the people here. They shouldn't be in here if they can't look after themselves. Some of them can't hold their cutlery properly and some of them were putting their food on the floor. It's awful. I don't remember how I ended up here. I just wish I could find some way to get back to my flat.

I went out last week. Did I tell you? I did. I went all the way to London on the train. It was night-time when I arrived and I didn't have anywhere to stay so I found a cupboard and a blanket and went in there to sleep where no one could find me. And then when it was light I woke up and... well I don't remember what I did next.

Dad was very good, you know. He never really had a proper job, but he and Mum worked hard and they saved enough to put down a deposit on a new house. Mum used to let the front room and the front bedroom to visitors in the summer to pay the rates. I had to share a bedroom with my two sisters. They had white metal twin beds with brass knobs at both ends and I had a black enamelled bed. All three of us in the same room. And Mum and Dad had a four-foot bed in the little bedroom. It must have been a bit off a squash.

Have you heard anything from my son? He never comes to visit me here, you know. I wonder if he knows where I am. I suspect with all that's gone on he just doesn't know where to find me. I know how it happened, you know. I went for a walk down by the canal near Vera's flat. We went down to look at some boathouses, or perhaps they were sheds, on the canal. My sister was with me, which was odd because I know she died years ago. And there we were, trapped in this hut and I kept telling my sister to get out the way so I could open the door and crawl out and go and get some help, but I couldn't get past her. I don't know what happened to the rest of the family though. Have you heard anything from my mother and father? Maybe you could go round and see if they are all right, but I suspect the house will be all shut up. It's such a good job my son managed to rescue these photographs otherwise we should have absolutely nothing to remember it all by, would we? Wasn't that a stroke of luck?

Ah, that's the bell for dinner time. I'm sorry you've had nowhere to sit other than perching there on the bed. Did I tell you they moved my bed again last night? It's the one complaint I have about this place.

HANNAH DEE

Hannah Dee is writing a memoir about her uncle, Michael MacLean [pseud], who was committed to Broadmoor in 1972 and detained in high-security psychiatric hospitals for several decades. Hannah has a background in publishing, research and social justice organising. She starts a creative writing PhD at Queen Mary University in September 2021.

hannahdee100@gmail.com

Broadmoor: 'It's A Good Home, Ain't It?'

Uncle Mikey had no idea what to expect when he arrived at Broadmoor. 'I thought I was going to a ward, with beds on it, a general hospital, like you see on TV,' he told me.[1] 'When I got there, they took me through the main gate, this big iron gate, walks me through and there's this senior nurse. "You've come to Broadmoor," he says to me. "Oh," I says. I smoked at the time and he said, "you can get a light on the ward" and I'm thinking I can sit on me bed and have a cigarette. Next thing you know four men turned up in white coats, hung over dark blue uniforms. They took me straight to the bathroom an' told me to get in this bath with two inches of cold water an' stood watching me strip off and dry meself. Then they said, "right, you're in there now" and banged me up in a strip room, with just a mattress and a piss pot in the corner. On the floor there was a plate with half a sausage and a dollop of potato – cold. "There's your tea," they said. And that was me introduction to it. Flippin 'eck, I thought, what's this?'

I knew what Mikey meant about the gate. I remember standing in front of it, age four, peering round Nan's crinkly vein-blue hand at the austere Victorian entrance, so vast that I could barely see the turret clock marking minutes above. As the visitors crowded round, a silence fell that dimmed all things familiar and magnified the terrible. Then the bell rang, a tiny door opened, and we shuffled through led by a man wearing a thick leather belt of jangle jar keys – just above my eye level. Mom remembers the long corridors, the size and bleakness of it. 'All them bars and windows with no escape. It was a really grim prospect to think of my brother staying in there.'[2] I just remember the way Mom and Dad seemed to shrink with every metal door that opened and locked, and a feeling of the world I knew being stripped away. In particular, it struck me that if these prison guards, if these 'screws', could kidnap my uncle indefinitely, and if my parents could do nothing about it, what was to stop them one day coming for me?

---

1 Mikey's words from interviews and conversations with the author 2019-2021.
2 Mom's words from interviews with the author 2019–21.

Ten years later I would see the same insipid green-yellow that coated Broadmoor's corridors on the walls of an adolescent unit as I arrived for my first psychiatric consultation. I'd been referred following a visit to the doctors after a dark, listless mood took hold and just refused to leave. Each night I begged the late hours to take me away and each morning I woke with a start, in anxious dread, sobbing and inconsolable. At first, I was relieved at getting a diagnosis of depression and the prospect of getting help, but my visit to Hollymoor Hospital soon put paid to that.

The introductory meeting with Mom, Dad and me was fairly perfunctory – apart from a small detail, mentioned in conversation, that anorexic residents could be force-fed. My eating disorder was pretty advanced by that point. I was around six stone and owner of a fiercely defended strategy of self-starvation, each day wrestling with the griping, biting mouths in my stomach. So as we walked through the corridors I kept glancing around the doors, looking for the room with the tubes, expecting at any moment to be confronted with the sight of a girl like me being strapped down and filled with liquid sludge, filled with sludge while thumbs, fingers and elbows held her down, draining her of integrity, until nothing of her own will was left.

A girl in a nightie was banging her head against the wall, mumbling and scuffing her feet against the worn carpet, dull thuds drifting over sad sagging chairs and plastic tables. As it was, the consultation didn't amount to much. The psychiatrist – a middle-aged man whose thin gnarly figure hunched at the shoulders – peered at me with eyes of glass. Who would I take with me to a desert island? he asked, from behind his desk across a distance that seemed as wide as the ocean. Of course, I knew *who* I would take, and *why*, but I couldn't possibly tell him.

Nevertheless, I came away from the hospital with what Auntie Betsy would call 'the fear of God' in me. It had been suggested to my parents that I might stay there, and I was terrified I would be taken away, just like my uncle. That I would be put inside and never get out. I felt utterly degraded and humiliated. Over and over, I kept thinking – do I have the gene, the dreaded mad gene? This was something me, my brother Luke and sister Ella were all afraid of, and although I've never asked him, I wonder if Luke was particularly worried since his reddish hair was a similar shade to Uncle Mikey's.

It was a shame really, that this small shred of hope of getting some relief from my depression turned out to be so disappointing, so utterly disassembling, because in the months that followed, the feeble line between myself and the wilderness completely disintegrated. Pain became such a fundamental part of living that escalating the attacks on my body seemed to be the only way to do something about it. I began washing incessantly, washing to erase the pain, to erase the self-loathing, to erase myself. I moved from soap to disinfectant to bleach, scrubbing and scratching at cracks and cuts on my hands and arms, stinging and burning. This was just one aspect of an obsessive-compulsive disorder which ruled over every waking moment – rules driven by a system of punishments and fear of catastrophe; rules which were tyrannical and ran completely out of my control; more bleach, or you'll go blind; check sockets, avoid explosion; don't touch, you'll be contaminated; check oven, the house might burn down; more bleach. Many years later my therapist suggested I might have been trying to cleanse myself of Broadmoor.

Strange these fears of madness were so dominant in our childhood, circling above us like birds of prey, since it was never really clear, what the gene was, or what illness Mikey suffered with. Within days of arriving at Broadmoor, a psychological test on Mikey concluded psychopathy was not supported, but an alternative label was difficult to determine. A review by one of Broadmoor's established psychiatrists noted that while doctors had previously agreed he was suffering from personality disorder, the episodes of psychosis suggested the voices Mikey complained of were a true auditory hallucination, and that he might well be a 'chronic paranoid schizophrenic'. No further comment was made on this significant revision to Mikey's original diagnosis, made just months before, by two medical practitioners whose signatures on a hospital order had consigned Mikey to indefinite psychiatric detention.

Progress reports by doctors and ward staff in the early months of Mikey's stay recorded his deterioration. One night it was reported that he had banged on his cell door, frightened after seeing faces on his cell wall and two men, one killing the other. Mikey told doctors he felt the voices commanding his thoughts were like two people, a young man and an older person. One voice spoke in Italian or Spanish which was disturbing because he couldn't make any sense of it. Mikey began to fear that people had been sent into Broadmoor to talk about him.

It hurt to think of Mikey sitting among the shadows and voices of men. The men who held him there, the men who brought him there, the men who hurt him in the past, the men he had hurt. 'It started one night,' Mikey told me. 'I had a nightmare, I was in the cell, looking up at the wall, and I could see all these little people walking past me, like little men. And I saw a murder. I saw somebody get stabbed. It was like reality.'

The cell Mikey had been taken to on his arrival was in the admission block, otherwise known as Norfolk House. There were seven male blocks in Broadmoor, each with three floors accommodating sleeping dormitories, strip cells, individual rooms and living quarters. Norfolk's charming name had come about following Superintendent Patrick McGrath's decision to modernise the place by replacing the block numbering scheme. A competition was put in the hospital's *Broadmoor Chronicle* and 'English Counties' selected as the winning idea. The seven male blocks were renamed Norfolk, Essex, Kent, Dorset, Gloucester, Monmouth, Cornwall, with York and Lancaster chosen for the female wing.[3] Broadmoor's graveyard, however, remained known by patients as Block 8 – the final destination for those buried on-site. 'The forgotten ones' Mikey calls them.

Norfolk House, like the other blocks, had its own peculiar history. It had been used as a prisoner of war camp during WW1 for German prisoners deemed mentally ill and dangerous.[4] In 1948, an insulin coma therapy unit was opened on the top floor of a disused dormitory. Here selected patients diagnosed with schizophrenia or depression would be injected with high doses of insulin, inducing coma states to break 'the thread of ordered ideas' and provide 'a short rest from... madness.'[5] The procedure involved the patient being given sixty injections over fourteen weeks, each one causing a rapid fall in glucose levels – flushing, sweating, salivating and sometimes fitting, before the inevitable coma. Nursing assistants would then insert long rubber tubes through the patient's nose or mouth, pouring glucose directly into their stomach to replace lost sugar and wake them. It was an extremely dangerous treatment, considered by its inventor, psychiatrist Manfred Sakel, to produce 'a clinical picture which would ordinarily be alarming.'[6] One observer of the procedure at Broadmoor suggested it was 'in the nature of an anteroom to death.'[7] Signed consent was required from patients and next of kin where possible, though Broadmoor wasn't the ideal setting for reaching voluntary agreements.

'When I got to Norfolk, I couldn't comprehend what was going on,' Mikey recalled. 'It was like I'd gone brain dead, like things were just happening.

3 D A Black, *Broadmoor Interacts*, London: Barry Rose Law Publishers, 2003, p.250.
4 Berkshire Records Office (BRO): D/H14/A6/2/5: *Broadmoor Correspondence File*. Accessed online 09.01.2021: https://berkshirevoiceswwi.wordpress.com/tag/broadmoor/.
5 Ralph Partridge, *Broadmoor*, London: Chatto & Windus, 1953, p.233.
6 Andrew Scull, *Madness in Civilization*, London: Thames & Hudson, 2016, p.310.
7 Ralph Partridge, ibid, p.233.

I was in shock, and I couldn't take it in. There was this funny smell, like an uncomfortable smell, that put you on edge, made you apprehensive. It was like something you couldn't tolerate, that you didn't want to be in. I'd never smelt anything like it in my life before, and I've never smelt it anywhere since, but when I went back to Norfolk years later, I could still smell it. It was like a smell of fear.

'The next day, everybody got up except me. Then about half past nine, the screws put me in a dressing gown, slippers and walked me into the main day room. Well, I decided to just sit there an' close my eyes. That went on for about three or four hours, and then they said you can get dressed now. They took me up to the storeroom, an' gave me clothes and then I went back to the day room. It was like a big room, chairs all around the walls and a TV and a radio in the middle, and there was another room next door, with a pool table, and that was it. That's what you got, two rooms, where you'd sit for hours on end every day. All the rest were cells. An' every time the screws walked in they were sayin' "it's a good home, ain't it?" They just kept on saying it all the time.'

NINA LESTER FINLEY

Nina Lester Finley is a disease ecologist from Seattle working at the intersection of human and ecosystem health. She is writing a book that explores ruptured relationships among humans, microbes, and ecosystems in the wake of colonialism and climate change. For more, visit www.ninafinley.com or follow @NinaFinley on Twitter.

ninafinley176@gmail.com

Flying North

The helicopter rose over Cambridge Bay. I pressed my forehead to the windshield and watched the Arctic town shrink to a speck in a cratered moonscape of jewel-tone pools. The largest held pistachio green at their centers, fanning out through shades of emerald, verdigris, and yellowish siskin at their edges. We veered south-west toward Karrak Lake, a remote outpost where I'd spend June and July attracting mosquitoes on a hunt for viruses that cause encephalitis, inflammation of the brain. The ocean below was coated in brilliant turquoise ice, spider-webbed with veins of white. In a trick of sunlight, the ice reminded me of a shallow tropical sea edged by white sand. I ached to know this place.

But the ache had a sharp edge, because this ice was melting. Every decade since 1979, when satellites began measuring sea ice, the autumn freeze has come five days later, and climate models predict ice-free summers as soon as 2032 if we keep emitting carbon dioxide as we do now.[1] The Canadian Arctic is warming three times faster than the global average. That's enough to collapse the permafrost under Cambridge Bay's stilt-legged houses, open vast polar oceans for oil drilling, and lure new wildlife north. Already, grizzlies are edging into polar bear territories and interbreeding to produce milky-brown hybrid cubs. A hunter shot the first wild nanulak – a combination of the Inuit word nanuk, for polar bear, and aklak, for grizzly – in 2006. I was here to investigate whether smaller wildlife, mosquitoes and their microbes, might be journeying north, too.

A two-hour flight over the tundra brought us to an island with a freshly painted outhouse, tents scattered across exposed rock, and aluminum skiffs bobbing among icebergs.

'Karrak Lake Research Station,' the pilot announced.

Eight researchers greeted us with cheers. Seven were there to study the million-strong Karrak Lake goose colony for the Canadian government. I shook hands with the eighth, Stephanie, a first-year PhD student. I'd be assisting with her project on vector-borne diseases – ailments caused by microbes that hitch rides in crawling, flying, biting things.

'So nice to finally meet you,' Stephanie gushed. Her blue eyes reminded me of the darker patches of sea ice. She showed me the station's plywood cabins. The largest was the kitchen, its gas stove surrounded by boots in puddles of melted snow. 'That's the laboratory for identifying mosquitoes,' she said, pointing to a microscope by the far wall. 'We're overdue for new information on Arctic mosquitoes. The last survey was in the '70s, and things have changed so much since then. Less ice, warmer days – who knows what species might be lurking up here!'

Of the world's 3,500 mosquito species, only a handful in the genus *Aedes* – pronounced like 'eighties' – can survive the Arctic climate. In mid-winter at Karrak Lake, temperatures regularly dip below -30°C, and the sun hovers weakly over the southern horizon for just a few hours a day. For two weeks in December, it fails to rise at all. It's hard to imagine any animal overwintering here, especially fragile insects that can't generate their own body heat or withstand strong winds. They've had to evolve creative coping strategies. Compared to their tropical cousins, Arctic mosquitoes are large, dark, and hairy. I've heard Alaskans joke that the mosquito is their state bird. These northern mosquitoes have developed the endearing habit of basking in patches of sunlight, stretching and preening like cats. They live for one year only, spending the first ten months as frozen eggs, and the final two in a frenzied rush to hatch, grow, eat, mate, and lay eggs of their own.

The cycle begins in early August, when females deposit eggs above the high-water line of boggy ponds. One species, *Aedes nigripes* – pronounced 'NIH-grih-pess' – lays eggs only while struck by direct sunlight, to ensure they'll be hit with the sun's first rays next spring.[2] The eggs are extraordinary for their ability to freeze and thaw undamaged. As soon as they're flooded by icy meltwater in June, the eggs hatch into aquatic larvae, giving them the nickname of 'snow-water mosquitoes.' At this stage, the larva's body is like a string of brown beads with a black head, spiked collar, and two-pronged tail through which it breathes. Wriggling in a near-freezing pond, it munches bacterial films that grow on muck for three weeks before it becomes a pupa and then a winged adult, ravenous for plant nectar and – if it's a female – the blood of any bird or mammal it can sniff. Once a female mosquito has mated and drunk blood, she's ready to lay eggs and repeat the cycle.

Although there are only a few mosquito species in the Arctic, the ones that live here are abundant. A person walking through the tundra in July can become coated in hundreds of the blood-suckers. They flit into your nose and eyes and ears until you think their high-pitched whine is coming from inside your own head. Diving beetles, lake whitefish, and Arctic char dine on the aquatic larvae, while migratory songbirds raise their chicks on the protein-rich adults. Luckily for me, mid-June was still chilly, and the mosquitoes were larvae. It would be a few weeks before the air warmed and *Aedes* engulfed the tundra in throbbing clouds.

On July 3rd, two weeks after I'd arrived, I gazed out the kitchen window, a mug of hot chocolate cooling in my hands. Ten hairy mosquitoes leered from the other side of the glass. I'd sighted the first one a few days before, a single insect wobbling on fresh wings. Maybe its mother had laid her eggs in a particularly sunny spot, allowing that individual to hatch early.

'Look at 'em all!' I called to Mel, a goose researcher here for her fifth season. Mel looked up skeptically from her book. She walked over, nursing a sore knee.

'Mosquitoes? I don't even *see* any yet,' she scoffed. 'This is nothing.' It was hard to tell when Mel was joking. I hoped she was.

I pulled on a mesh jacket with a full-face hood and latex gloves for my first day of mosquito trapping. Bug spray was forbidden. The research protocol had me as both collector and bait. At a designated spot, I recorded the air temperature and wind speed, then stood with arms outstretched. Already, mosquitoes were gathering. They followed the warmth of my body and the smell of my exhaled carbon dioxide – odorless to my weaker nose – and even the scent of the bacteria on my skin.

I swooped my net in figure-eights for ten minutes, gently transferring the mosquitoes into a gauze-sided box. The mosquitoes' probing proboscises couldn't penetrate my latex gloves or mesh jacket, so I had only a few welts on my left wrist where the cuff had uncinched.

Back behind the kitchen – the goose researchers had vetoed bringing the mosquitoes inside – I switched on the Bug Vac, a kind of custom hairdryer for sucking mosquitoes into plastic vials. Today's sample filled one-third of a vial with hundreds of jostling bodies. I dropped it into the freezer and waited for the mosquitoes to die.

Mel had not been joking. Within days, every ten-minute sample filled multiple vials. The freezer got crowded. One morning, I went skinny-dipping in the lake, managing a few strokes before my lips turned blue. Seconds after I'd pulled myself ashore, thousands of mosquitoes had settled on my exposed skin. I will never forget looking down. It was as if I had wrapped myself in a pulsing gray towel.

Grizzlies were an ever-present danger at Karrak Lake – I carried bear spray whenever I left a cabin – but the grizzly is not the world's deadliest animal, not even close. That title belongs to the mosquito. Grizzlies take around one human life each year. Mosquitoes, and the diseases they spread, claim a million.[3] Nearly all these deaths occur in the tropics. Up north, only two mosquito-borne microbes, the Jamestown Canyon and snowshoe hare viruses, are known to infect humans, and they've caused fewer than 300 cases of encephalitis in Canada since the 1970s.[4] That's due, in part, to one simple fact: the Arctic is cold.

For a microbe, catching a ride inside a mosquito is a harrowing experience. Warm temperatures make it a little easier. The reasons lie deep in the gut of mosquito biology. It all begins when a female mosquito bites an infected host – a human with dengue, say, or an Arctic fox with encephalitis. The mosquito pricks, gulps, and swallows, storing the blood in its midgut. Some microbes from that blood pierce the midgut's mucosal lining to replicate. At each step, microbes must overcome the mosquito's immune system, digestive juices, and in-cell defense mechanisms. Finally, the cleverest and strongest survivors enter the mosquito's salivary gland and run one more gauntlet, down its thin proboscis to the bloodstream of its next victim. The process can take weeks.[5]

This is where temperature comes in. Like a researcher snuggled in a sleeping bag on a frosty morning, cold microbes get sluggish. Some scientists hypothesize that Arctic mosquitoes carry so few diseases because the summers are simply too cold and short. The few weeks that Arctic mosquitoes spend in their adult form might not be long enough for microbes to wind through a mosquito's tissues to a new host, especially when cool temperatures slow them down. But, due to climate change, Arctic summers get longer and warmer every year. Warm microbes are full of pizzazz: they replicate fast and scurry through the mosquito in less time. At 25°C, a dengue virus spends an average of fifteen days in a mosquito. Crank the temperature up 5°C, and the virus moves through in less than a week.[6] Dengue and most other mosquito-borne viruses are restricted to the tropics, but warmth is spreading.

It's impossible to say exactly how mosquito-borne diseases will change in the future. There are too many factors – rainfall, vegetation, public health infrastructure, urbanization, access to medical care, and many others. But it is clear that cold-blooded insects and their microbes, on the whole, do better in a warmer world. Over the past two decades in Canada, the incidence of mosquito-borne viruses increased by ten percent.[7] Scientific models predict that malaria will cause an additional 60,000 deaths every year between 2030 and 2050 due to climate change,[8] and that six billion people will be at risk of dengue fever by 2080.[9] The expansion of mosquitoes and their microbes is a primary reason why the World Health Organization considers climate change the greatest public health threat of the twenty-first century.

It took three days for my first vial of mosquitoes to die. When at last they stopped twitching, I sifted out the males by their woolly antennae, used for tracking females' wingbeats, and brought the females to Stephanie at the microscope.

'Want to see how I tell the species apart?' she offered.

I leaned over the eye-pieces and adjusted the focus until one hairy mosquito swam into view. I could make out the knobby joints of its knees, the trailing fringe on its wings, the obsidian scales on its humped back. At this magnification, it looked like a sleeping dragon. Stephanie tapped one of the mosquito's legs with her forceps.

'See that spine growing backward out of its foot?' she asked. 'That's the tarsal claw. And see how it curves abruptly, not gradually? That's how I can tell it's *Aedes impiger*.' She emphasized the species name, 'IM-pih-jer,' Latin for energetic and active. I leaned back and rubbed my eyes, dizzy from the microscope's lenses. Alone in its dish, the crumbled insect looked anything but energetic.

So far, Stephanie had identified three species, all typical Arctic mosquitoes in the genus *Aedes*. It didn't make headlines, but it was good news for human health. Any day, she could peer through those lenses and encounter an unfamiliar crook in the tarsal claw, perhaps, or an unexpected pattern of obsidian scales – a new arrival in the North, and whatever microbes it might be carrying within.

1. Jahn, A., Kay, J. E., Holland, M. M. & Hall, D. M. How predictable is the timing of a summer ice-free Arctic? Predicting a summer ice-free Arctic. *Geophys. Res. Lett.* 43, 9113–9120 (2016).
2. Corbet, P. S. & Danks, H. V. Egg-laying habits of mosquitoes in the high arctic. *Mosq. News* 35, 8–14 (1975).
3. Bates, C. Would it be wrong to eradicate mosquitoes? *BBC News Magazine* (2016).
4. Drebot, M. Emerging mosquito-borne bunyaviruses in Canada. *Can. Commun. Dis. Rep.* 41, 117–123 (2015).
5. Tabachnick, W. Nature, Nurture and Evolution of Intra-Species Variation in Mosquito Arbovirus Transmission Competence. *Int. J. Environ. Res. Public. Health* 10, 249–277 (2013).
6. Chan, M. & Johansson, M. A. The Incubation Periods of Dengue Viruses. *PLoS ONE* 7, e50972 (2012).
7. Ludwig, A. *et al.* Increased risk of endemic mosquito-borne diseases in Canada due to climate change. *Can. Commun. Dis. Rep.* 45, 91–97 (2019).
8. World Health Organization. *Climate change and health.* www.who.int/news-room/fact-sheets/detail/climate-change-and-health (2018).
9. Messina, J. P. *et al.* The current and future global distribution and population at risk of dengue. *Nat. Microbiol.* 4, 1508–1515 (2019).

NOTE – Illustration and photograph are by the author, who retains the copyright. Names have been changed.

ROBERT GARNER

Robert Garner is Emeritus Professor of Politics at the University of Leicester. He has published widely on party politics, environmental politics and the politics and philosophy of animal rights. He is currently writing a novelistic account of the 1945 British General Election.

rwg2@le.ac.uk
www.robert-garner.com

Extracts from the Diary of an Academic

OCTOBER

2nd

It's official. I have formally taken over, for a three-year term, the role of head of a medium-sized social science department in a medium-sized Midlands university in a medium-sized city. It sounds grand but in reality it's 'Buggins's turn'. At the departmental meeting, I was met with faces etched with a combination of sympathy and relief. That's three years of my life I'll never get back, a life that will be dominated by administration and a much-reduced teaching and research load.

10th

Visited by three students today who have, justifiably, complaints. I try (and succeed I think) to maintain an outward air of interest and concern, whilst masking the inner heartsink feeling that comes with the realisation that I am the one who will have to deal with resolving these complaints myself. The buck stops with me.

11th

Explain to Professor D that it is not appropriate to greet a student knocking on his door with the words 'fuck off', that it wasn't appropriate twenty years ago, let alone in an era of high tuition fees. He begrudgingly articulates the word 'fine'. However, his facial expression says 'you fuck off.'

12th

Explain to Dr S that it is not appropriate in a first-year undergraduate lecture to ask all the virgins to move to the front. Threaten to report him to the 'Student Experience' Committee chaired by the vice chancellor (VC) if he transgresses again.

13th

Explain to Dr F that living sixty miles away from the campus does not justify coming to work two days a week and missing an office hour. She complains that I am breaching her 'fundamental commuter rights.'

24th

Explain to an undergraduate that he's unlikely to get permission to go to Iraq and interview people about their views on Islamic Fundamentalism for his dissertation. Disappointed at this news he replies, 'What about Romford?'

25th

Spending an inordinate amount of time sitting in the departmental office. Notice an 'RG Memorial Chair' label where I am sitting. Much guffawing among the professional service staff. Point out to the room that I am not dead yet!

NOVEMBER

2nd

Attend a training session for heads of department. Given a 'stress ball' in the course pack. The VC, a cross between Stalin and Liberace, arrives, eyes the ball with wry disdain and snorts: 'You are going to need more than that.'

5th

Meeting with a pro-vice chancellor who is 'tasked' with the job of relocating Dr M from a cognate social science department. They are refusing to have her anymore for some unspecified, presumably disciplinary, reasons. I ask for their record of her employment only to be told they have 'lost the file.' Given the department's staff shortages, agree to take her on anyway. More preoccupied at the time with the propensity for 'verbing' amongst university managers, based on the principle that if you can't find an existing verb to describe what you're doing, just 'verbify' the nearest noun. In recent meetings, I've been 'tasked' to 'table' this, 'calendar' that and 'action' the other. I have been 'onboarded' to a variety of committees. I wonder if I can 'Houdini' my way out of this job sometime soon. Have to 'workshop' that idea.

22nd
Conducting a fire safety inspection in the department. Go into one colleague's office and notice an electric bar heater perched on top of newspapers. Colleague sheepishly promises to deal with it.

DECEMBER

6th
Attending Senate, the university's governing body. Looked through fingers as a professor of English put his head above the parapet and challenged the VC's position that we should ignore English language requirements when recruiting graduate students. Duly shot off.

18th
Major *faux pas*. Catch sight of student handing in an essay with only minutes to spare. Say to him 'you are leaving it a bit late' only to see him limping away with difficulty. Subsequently hear that the lift to the tenth floor wasn't working. Feel even worse.

JANUARY

15th
Having new bookshelves put in my tenth-floor office. University maintenance man tells me that he can't put them on the outside walls for fear that drilling will destabilise the building. Rather perturbed with the idea that the high-rise building I spend nigh on a hundred per cent of my working life in could be so easily weakened. Spend the rest of the day convinced that I can see the walls moving.

17th
First meeting of the year, a university research panel chaired by the VC. We are finalising our submission to the so-called Research Excellence Framework (REF). This is a Government-mandated exercise where all of our activities – research environment, impact and outputs (books and articles produced by members of the department) – over the past five years or so are graded (one being the lowest and four the highest) by panels of 'experts' (i.e. fellow academics). A final aggregate score for the department

is then arrived at. Every subject area in every higher education institution has to go through this. This scrutiny of research has occurred since 1986 and is part of successive governments' commitment to making universities more accountable (the – false – assumption being that if left to their own devices, academics will get away with doing very little).

A relatively small proportion of the university's income comes from this exercise but it is regarded as a crucial indicator of status. In reality, for departments with any research credibility, an overall rating of under three is regarded as pretty catastrophic. In the meeting, I confidently predict that we will get above a three. The VC doesn't look convinced but what else am I supposed to say? Admit that we are not very good?

FEBRUARY

27th
Find out that Dr M has taken out a grievance procedure against me. Claims that I told her I would give her a hard time if she doesn't toe the line. Luckily, I have kept her e-mail in which she thanked me for a very productive meeting (strangely enough because I *did* tell her I would give her a hard time).

MARCH

8th
Professor M brings in a much-appreciated cake for International Women's Day. The men in the department take the biggest portions.

12th
Meeting of heads of department in the faculty. We agree to pay postgraduates to paint offices in our building. Think the post-nuclear look has had its day.

15th
Told that our departmental secretary gets louder and more gushing as the day goes on. Insists upon calling everyone 'my lover'. Investigate after she has gone home. Suspicious smell of alcohol in her coffee mug.

19th

Catch Dr S from Psychology bringing a mug of coffee for the departmental secretary. Later in the day I take a sniff in said mug and, sure enough, it is some sort of alcohol. Consider what I should do about it. Tricky issue. Resolve to keep it under review.

28th

Postgraduates make a good job of painting offices. Resist the urge to tell them if they researched as well as they painted they'd spend less than six years obtaining their doctorates.

29th

Get phone call from the VC. Explains he has been making unannounced and anonymous calls to departments pretending to be a parent of a student. Wishes to pass on congratulations to our departmental secretary for her 'lively and friendly manner.'

APRIL

15th

Job is getting me down. Start looking at positions elsewhere. See at least three professorships (or chairs) I could apply for at other universities. Mention this to a friend and he says, helpfully, that rather than three chairs why don't I just go for a sofa. I change the subject.

MAY

9th

To mark the end of the teaching year, take my final year students for a drink in the Students' Union bar. An excellent group who have been enthusiastic and, for the most part, talented. They seem to be greatly amused buying me a succession of green shots on the grounds that the course I have been teaching has an environmental theme. Stagger back to hotel.

10th

Informed that a Graduate Teaching Assistant has been saying to his students, with great envy, how I must be 'coining it in' as head of department.

See him later in my office and remind him that, even if it is true (which it's not), he should not be making such personal comments in seminars. Secretly pleased that he, and some of the students, think I am so affluent. Strut home with a smile on my face.

14th

Departmental secretary announces she wants to take early retirement. Support her decision with some relief and not a little regret. All told, she has been an excellent colleague.

21st

Find out that the Estates Department hasn't taken too kindly to postgraduates being used to improve the décor. In what quickly became known as 'Emulsiongate', all heads are given a dressing-down and warned about future behaviour.

JUNE

11th

Major marking catastrophe avoided. Introduced a multiple-choice exam this year for my course. Thought it would be a good idea to take marks off for incorrect answers to stop students being rewarded for guessing. Realise it was a BAD idea when one candidate scores minus twenty. Hurriedly convene a meeting of colleagues to abandon negative marking.

JULY

10th

Attend graduation ceremony. Dressed like an inflated custard cream. Very hot on the stage and hands stinging with the constant clapping required. Conscious of beginning to sweat. Mood lifted by an extraordinary speech by a well-known comedian who is receiving (for some reason) an honorary doctorate. He finishes by telling the graduating students: 'You go out there and have yourselves a fucking good life.' Noted with enormous satisfaction the VC flinching as the students roared their approval. At the reception afterwards, have to tell an overseas student that I can't accept a ceremonial sword as a gift.

AUGUST

12th

Heading to France to stay at partner's parents' place for a well-earnt break. Should be focusing on my research and writing but much too tired to do that. First trip away with new baby. On the Eurostar, I ask, 'Do we need a passport for him?' Mouths open. Decide that it would be helpful to have one. I suggest, half seriously, hiding baby in a suitcase, but quickly realise that didn't go down too well. Baby is wonderfully well-behaved, gurgling happily and periodically lulled into sleep by the rhythmic sound of the train. Get to Paris. Discover the French aren't really bothered if we have a passport for him or not. Partner is an immigration lawyer which helps in these types of circumstances. Make call to get some relevant documentation for the return journey.

OCTOBER

5th

On my way back from a conference in York. Get off at Peterborough to change trains. Shocked to see VC is waiting to get off too. Try to hide but he spots me and invites me to travel back with him in the university's chauffeur-driven car. One hour of agony. Try to engage in small talk. Confidently predict (again) that the department will get at least a three in the REF. He tells me that on the results day he is hosting a lunchtime drinks reception for heads of department.

NOVEMBER

17th

Attending university-wide meeting of heads of department and senior management. Head of HR starts meeting by showing a YouTube video of a girl being ridiculed by some boys for the way she throws a ball. There is general murmuring that this stereotyping is unacceptable. Dean of the Arts then gets up and announces 'I'm ashamed' as though it's his fault. After an hour we (briefly) discuss the university's financial crisis and the possible need for compulsory redundancies.

DECEMBER

18th
Wake up with a sense of impending doom. REF result due today. The results go to the VC first. Get a phone call from him mid-morning. Tells me we have got below a three and not to come to the drinks reception he's organised for heads of department. Spent rest of the day in the pub drowning my sorrows.

20th
VC tells me it is likely that the department will have to lose some posts. Start negotiating Dr S's transfer to the Psychology Department.

21st
Home for much needed break. Less than two years left in this job now.

CONSTANCE HARRIS

Constance Harris is an Irish writer who worked in film and fashion and is a shamanic healer of the Q'ero lineage. Her first novel was longlisted in the Irish Writers Centre Novel Fair 2021. She is working on a collection of short stories and a memoir-based book on fashion, healing and change.

constanceharris09@gmail.com

These Hills of Dark Containment
Extract from a non-fiction short story

I was to meet the owner at 11am. The property was an old farmhouse on 1.35 acres at an exceptionally keen price. There had to be a catch. I hoped it was a catch I could deal with.

In these parts, I am what is known as a 'blow-in'. Live here but not from here. Blow-in makes one sound like a ship that lost its course and washed up on one of the Atlantic-made ragged shore lines which defines this part of west Cork. Even if you were born here but your parents or grandparents weren't, you're a blow-in. Locals' memories are long about such things. Never fully accepted. Never included in their secrets.

My car bounced terrifyingly along the bockety curving boreen with a mohawk of wild grass running through its centre and potholes like old cannon balls to best challenge the integrity of a car's chassis. Finally I located the old farm. It was nestling beneath a high hedge that marked the property's boundary, and which also hid it from its neighbours. There was a near-vertical drive, it was that steep, down to the farmyard. I made the turn carefully and drove down slow, taking in as much of the place as I could, for once I parked up I would not get a chance to survey it unsupervised again.

The house was a traditional modest two-storey Irish farmhouse built in the 1880s, forty years after what is known as The Great Famine, a dividing line in Irish history. It had a front door with a small window on each side and three small windows above. At some stage, probably in the 1960s, someone built an ugly single-storey extension to its side. To the front of the house was cement ground across from which stood a much older, tiny, stone building – a pre-famine house.

While I parked my car, out a side door of the ugly extension came a tall, old man. He had a distinguished bearing though he was dressed in an ancient thick sweater tucked into faded work dungarees. A flat cap on his head looked as worn as he. White eyebrows on a pale, wrinkled face were that thick I couldn't properly see his eyes. But he must have been handsome when young, for he was strong-faced in old age. He walked hesitantly towards me.

'Mr Donovan?' I asked. I extended my hand.

He looked at me as if surprised that I was there, but nodded his head in typical country acknowledgement, eventually taking my hand. As if it were a strange thing to be doing. It wasn't an energetic clasp such as men usually do – city men, young men. More a light holding. His hands were big and dry, working hands. And clean. Everything about him was aged and worn looking, but clean.

So far he'd said barely a word. No 'You're here to view the house, aren't you?' No 'Welcome, welcome, we've been expecting you.' I began to doubt I was in the right place.

'This is Ballyboreen Farm? I have it right? Mr Connolly the estate agent arranged that I could visit this morning?'

Again a nod.

'Is it yourself is to show me around? Is your wife here? I was told you and your wife live here.'

'No.' Silence for a long moment. 'Herself isn't here. She had to go into the town.'

'Ah. OK,' I said. And wondered what to do. I was unexpectedly alone in a remote place with an old man. I grew up wary of old men, especially country old men. They could be odd. From living alone, and too isolated. Inside, I gave myself a talking to: he was a nice old fella. Of course he was. And the undeniable fact – if I wanted to see this house, I had to make a leap of faith.

Looking at him, he seemed as unsure as I was. We'd both been quiet.

'I suppose... you'd like a look around?' He eventually said. To city people this kind of question would seem a bit ridiculous – I had a formal appointment. But in rural Ireland, and especially in Cork where class, as well as country wariness, colours everything, such a statement was the golden ticket: I was to be allowed to cross the threshold.

'Yes,' I said. 'Thank you.'

He nodded again and walked me to the side door he had come out of a few minutes before but then seemed unsure whether he should go in first, or I. He opened the door and stepped back, indicating I should go before him. I stepped into a stark, dark, bleak space that was evidently their kitchen. In Ireland, heart and hearth are closely aligned and the kitchen is where they reside. Not so here. Aluminium grey single-glazed windows sat above a stainless steel sink set over cupboards that were ugly the day they were put in and hadn't been improved any since. Gloss-painted (for ease of keeping clean?) walls of a bilious colour. Once brown, now nothing-coloured lino on the ground. A battered kitchen table and two chairs.

'It's a grand big kitchen,' I said. It was the best I could think of. He nodded. Said nothing. I noticed a door at the end. 'Is that the way into the main house?' Another nod. Taking that as permission, I walked through the door and found myself in a traditional Irish living room: scorched mantelpiece from a well-used fireplace; tongue and groove wood-panelled walls and ceilings discoloured by years of smoke from turf fires; worn tartan blankets covered two couches so used their seats had sunk down near to sitting on the floor themselves. There was a clock and a faded Christ. Everything was so tired, so discoloured from age and smoke, that I had an impression of haze more than anything.

'This is a fine room,' I said. 'A good size.'

He looked around it slowly as if seeing it for the first time. I could think of nothing more to say and I realised there was nothing he was going to say. Or that he was going to lead the way in this showing of his home. In the presence of his silence, my behaviour was becoming a kind of performance: I'd point out something, he'd nod, then we could move on. But his quietness began to get to me. I decided to get through the rest of the viewing as quickly as possible. I went through another door which took me into the hall but the front door didn't open. There was only one way out. Behind him.

'Do you... I suppose you will be wanting to see upstairs?' he said, indicating the narrow wooden steps going upwards. What I wanted was this whole experience over. I lamented that there was no estate agent present to prattle about the property and distract me from my fear.

I started up the stairs, which were narrow and boxed in at the sides, typical of old Irish houses where staircases seemed an afterthought. From my ascending vantage point, I saw three open doors and the legs of the beds within. Suddenly the silence, the isolation, the enclosed nature of the staircase and where we were heading, got to me. I panicked. I turned around thinking just to get out – but he was right behind me. Close behind.

But as I stopped, so did he. He looked around, then pointed to a small, rickety-looking window set just above to bring some light into the stairwell. An Infant of Prague, a religious statue of an overdressed male toddler, sat to the side of the windowsill, now faded and finished like everything else in this house.

'This is good, isn't it? It's good to have a window here?' he said. It was his first unsolicited uttering. He turned away from me and patted the window. Almost proudly. 'I put that in... I can't remember when... Would you like to see it open?' He looked back at me as if he felt he had finally recognised what language I spoke. Houses and their features. He would give it a go.

'It is. It is good to have a window there.' I replied. I could hear the shake in my voice. He fiddled with the window's latch. I worked to calm myself down.

I decided I wasn't going to waste time doing any more of the 'house drama' stuff that I had enacted down below out of politeness. I wanted out. I went up the last few steps and stepped into the main bedroom, I glanced around ready to run at the slightest shift in the air. I saw him look in. Whether it was that he knew I was nervous, or that it had struck him that we were a man and a woman, strangers, alone in what could well have been his marital bedroom, he remained out on the landing.

The room was bare. White walls, a bed and bedside locker. A dark wardrobe. A crucifix. Unvarnished floorboards – well swept. No flowery bedspreads, curtains or cushions typical of female occupation were in evidence. I glanced into another room – and couldn't take it anymore. I was now wondering about their lives. His and his wife's. I wondered what kind of living went on here. It felt barren. Grim. I began to feel for this tall old man who was so careful and reserved.

'Thank you,' I said and headed directly down the stairs. Glancing over my shoulder, I saw him look back towards the bedrooms then follow down slowly. I didn't wait for him. I rushed through the house.

Out in the yard, in the sunshine and space, I felt better. I would do this, finish the viewing.

'May I have a look around the yard?' I asked him when he came out. I saw a bit of garden over towards the side, indicating the far side of the house. Again he said nothing and feeling more acclimatised to his manner, I walked to where I wanted to go, he following. It was a truly small lawn, but beautifully tended. There wasn't a weed or a bump anywhere. Having struggled with lawns all my life, my appreciation of its perfection was genuine. 'With what do you cut this lawn?' I asked. 'Have you a push-a-long?' He seemed bemused by my question but responded with a nod indicating 'yes'.

'I have an old lawnmower there, in the shed,' he said.

'I thought so,' I replied. 'You can always tell a lawn that has been cut by an old lawnmower. It always looks better. Don't you think?'

He seemed to consider this theory. As we stood in silence looking over the perfect box of green he had tended – probably for his entire life – he visibly relaxed. We walked over and looked into the big metal open shed which must once have housed his tractor but now stood cleaned out, as everything was I came to realise. I chattered on a bit about loving gardening and how I preferred to grow fruit and vegetables to flowers; that I had better success with them, and that was why I was looking for a bit of land.

He walked me around a lovely hedge that he was proud to show me because of the variant it was – challenging to grow in this clime – beside which a little stream ran. As we walked, he began to speak more. He talked about plants he had cultivated. We talked of streams and the merits of wells. He offered to show me where the best beehives thrive up on a hillock. It was clear that he loved every bit of this farm that he tended.

'Why are you selling?' I blurted as we walked up the hill. 'I mean...' I faltered. Suddenly aware that I had asked an extremely personal question: land and Irish people are something you do not get between. But I couldn't stop now I had started. 'You love the land.'

His pace did not alter, nor did he indicate I had asked anything.

Then. 'The wife wants to move. To Bantry.'

'To be nearer your daughter?' I responded. He said nothing.

I imagined this man, so clearly at one with the land, being uprooted to live in a built-up terraced house in a car-filled town. I thought – he'll be dead within the year. I wondered at his wife. This house of hers that I had been all around. This house that was absent of beauty or warmth. Hard worn, unadorned, harsh.

'Tis her farm.'

Tar isteach is Gaelic for 'come inside'. It's a phrasal verb. But in this part of the country it's also used as a noun: a 'come in' marries into a farm. He brings no land of his own. He has no sovereignty, no jurisdiction. Behind his back and for generations later, he'll be referred to as the '*tar isteach*'.

This gentle man was one such. I began to understand it all. His life. Married in. Granted no power. No worth. No say. The 'come in'.

At the end of his life. T'is her farm. No home for a blow-in.

AZADEH HASHEMIAN

Azadeh Hashemian was born in 1979 in Tehran, Iran, and so her life history has always been tied to its politics. Inside this life, she looks for ordinary people's stories that resonate with people of the outer world. Azadeh's short stories and translated pieces have been published in Iranian magazines and also in Silk Routes, a three-year project by Iowa Writing Program in central Asia. She is currently working on a memoir based on the scarf and its influence on Iranian women's daily lives.

azadeh.hashemian@gmail.com

Scarf Story

One autumn afternoon in my fourth grade, our teacher was called out of the classroom. When she returned, she announced that she had to leave earlier than usual. We could paint or talk or do homework, she said, as long as our noise did not bother other classes.

Our school worked in two shifts: mornings and afternoons, which would change fortnightly. This was the last hour of the afternoon shift. The classroom was already dark, since it was a rainy autumn day and any light that would ordinarily come in from outside was obscured. Two years earlier the glass in our windows had been painted over in white, as they had been in all girls' schools' windows due to new Islamic rules following the 1979 revolution. With teacher gone, some girls wrote on the blackboard, others played or chattered. The humming sound of girls became louder with each minute that passed. My friend and I were playing Squares and Dots. We would laugh as we each tried to stop the other completing the square.

Suddenly my laugh echoed in the dead silent class. I turned my head to see the Governess standing at the door, staring at us. She was thin. Very thin. Bony cheeks, bony forehead, even bony eyebrows, all framed in a tight, black scarf, revealing not a single strand of hair. In a long, black manteaux and a black sweater. It was a cold day.

'I am disappointed. I had counted on you to stay calm when your teacher has a problem. You are nine years old,' she said stretching the vowel.

We did not blink or breathe.

'Don't you understand that other classes are studying? Why do you make so much noise?'

She sat on the teacher's desk. Behind her, above the blackboard, was a portrait of Imam Khomeini smiling: 'You are my hope, you primary school kids,' read the text under the photo. My desk was in the second row, and I could see the loose black stockings she wore over her bony ankles as she dangled her legs in the air.

Did we understand what it meant for a girl to be nine years old? she asked the silent class. We were mature in God's eyes. Since the day we turned nine, we were accountable for our actions. Not so boys. Boys were considered mature at the age of fifteen. Did we understand that? That was because girls were wiser. But what about us? Our teacher could not leave us to ourselves for a minute. We, at the age of nine, while mature in God's eyes, could not keep quiet for an hour.

And she was hearing things. About us. Yes. She knew that some of us went out without the proper hijab. She just felt responsible, she said. That she must tell us this because our parents were being neglectful. In the presence of male strangers, we had to wear scarves. We were not children any more. If we went to parties in skirts, if a man saw our legs, we would be hanged from one strand of hair of that leg. Did we know what awaited us if we missed daily prayers? A hot pot of boiling tar. Yes. We'd be boiling there forever.

With her long fingers, she stirred the imagined boiling pot on her lap. The veins on the back of her hand shone under the flickering fluorescent lamp. The rain beat on the window pane and mingled with the sudden sound of the school bell. The Governess slid off the table. She would pray that God could forgive us, she said.

Out in the rain, Maman was waiting with an umbrella. She had come to protect me from getting drenched by the rain. But to my young mind, newly informed by the Governess's words, she seemed so vulnerable. What was she going to do with all those missed daily prayers? How come she had not told me about all these dangers? The street smelled of rain and my face felt warm against her hand. I looked around and saw other mothers. Maman's scarf was looser than everyone else's. And no one was out in a skirt, except her. How she would deal with that agony of the boiling tar, I wondered.

Around the same time, something happened that made me even more concerned about my newly-learned beliefs. On a winter day, a friend stuck her mouth to my ear and said in a quiet, hushed voice that she had seen one of our classmates 'bareheaded' in the street. Then she stood in front of me to see the effect of her news on me. The scarf cloth near my ear was hot from her breath.

'Bareheaded?' I looked into her eyes. I had not heard this word before.

'Yes. No scarf,' my friend said.

I tried to make a most surprised face for her appreciation, as I thought of myself going everywhere (except for school) without the hijab. What if they saw me in the street in a T-shirt and jeans? A black scarf was part of the school uniform, but I needed a coloured scarf, like the ones Maman had, for other places. Arriving home, I announced this to her.

'What for?' Maman said.

'To cover my hair,' I said. 'We are nine. Nine is the age to cover your hair.'

'Bullshit,' she said, 'you don't need to. You'll have enough time to cover your hair when you grow up.'

What I did not tell Maman was that I feared not only God and his hellfire, but also the spies that our Governess claimed to have all around the school and that were also likely to be all around the neighbourhood. I would never tell these things to my parents since I knew it would evoke a fierce rage in them. Baba, my father, loathed what he called 'teaching superstition' at schools, and Maman detested the hijab. Only a few years ago you could wear whatever you pleased, she said, they could not make a kid wear what she did not like.

'I am not a kid,' I would announce, 'and I like to wear a scarf.' A scarf would make me feel grown-up and help me fit in and be more similar to my school friends, I was thinking.

For several days, Maman resisted my demands to conform. Then she conceded: she bought me a scarf. A white one with colourful pom-poms all around it. A childish style, I felt. But better than walking around bareheaded in the streets.

This was the first time that we had a disagreement on one another's outfits, but not the last time. It seems to me now that she could define the world to me in a way that my father would never be able to. Maman told me her history with the hijab and defined her position (and even mine despite my resistance) towards it. In 1936, Reza Shah, the king at that time, decreed that women must not wear the veil, intending it to be an act to liberate women. But in practice it resulted in many women being imprisoned in their homes and deprived of attending school because their families believed in wearing the hijab.[1] Though the next king, Reza Shah's son, relieved the pressure on women by making the hijab optional in the 60s, unveiling became synonymous with support of the kingdom, whilst both men and women took up unveiling as part of the anti-monarchy movement. People began to embrace veiling as they more and more rebelled against the kingdom. This trend towards more modesty, at least as regards women's wear, grew further after the 1979 revolution until 1983, when wearing of the veil was officially legislated.

1 All dates and historical facts about the hijab are obtained from 'Hijab and the Intellectuals.' Nooshin Ahmadi Khorasani, (self-published, 2009).

Unlike her friends, Maman never wore a scarf voluntarily, either before or after the revolution. She relished her freedom from the veil during the kings' rule and after the revolution she continued with her preference. Religious fever was like an epidemic at the time and she had never been a person to follow feverish feelings. Even after the legislation of the veil, when she had to acquiesce, I could feel her reluctance. And I did not like it. I liked her to fit in with other mothers in the neighbourhood. I was also worried about her. I would look at her crossed legs at a party and think of her male cousins, who were not Mahram,[2] according to Islam. I stared at her legs' tiny invisible hairs. Would it be possible to hang someone from that? I would think as I remembered that gloomy autumn afternoon at school. When a classmate had commented that a single hair might not be able to tolerate a woman's weight, the Governess had rolled her eyes and said: 'Do you think God is not able to think of making it so? He has created us himself, and he knows better.'

Soon I would be a teenager and we would change places in watching one another's clothes. In many families, teenagers' clothing becomes a point of tension, but in our case, I started commenting on my mother's clothes before she started to comment on mine. She did not like it. She would look at me – now reaching her chest – eyebrows raised, 'When did you grow up, little girl? You cannot comment on what I wear.' But again, if she was going to meet my teacher, dressed in a glossy pair of stockings, I would encourage her to wear something to cover her legs and that only made things worse between us.

In one way or another, whether it was decreed by the Government or decided by ourselves, what we wore became a wall between my mother and me. What was once passionately argued, now became a silent war, and one as difficult to end as any.

---

[2] A woman needs to use the hijab only in the presence of men who are not her Mahram, i.e. immediate family members like father, grandfather, son, grandson, and brother.

LALYA LLOYD

Lalya Lloyd won the *TLS*'s Student Centenary Writing Award while an undergraduate at Cambridge. She has worked as a book reviewer and taught Classics at Eton College. For the last 12 years, she has lived in a blue-plaqued house in Kensington and is writing about its history and inhabitants.

lalya.lloyd@gmail.com
@lalyalloyd

Church Street

When I first meet Dick Horsley, he has five children, ten grandchildren and two great-grandchildren. That's not how he counts them up, though. He says, 'I have 17 descendants,' and smiles broadly as he runs out of fingers. In the decade I've known him, he – or rather his female relatives – have added about a score more, and it hurts my head to keep track of them.

It takes me ages to meet most of his family. Although he lives in a sprawling Kensington mansion with about ten bedrooms (one of which I lease from him at a modest sum), his children and grandchildren don't often drop by. On the other hand, he is never lonely. He runs a publishing business from the ground floor mezzanine – a converted artist's studio with a nine-foot high west-facing window – and there is an almost constant stream of visitors. In the summer I am sometimes invited to drink sherry under the purple wisteria with a succession of Dick's friends. One day, on his way in for a publishers' meeting, a famous politician compliments me on my pyjamas.

Dick has fixed ideas on love and marriage. 'I said to my daughters,' – he effervesces one summer evening by the light of a flickering candle, his syrupy voice, in low patrician tones, gliding across the dining table over the remnants of tunny fish, dark berries and wine glasses, to find an ear in us all – 'I said to them: "You can marry whomsoever you choose. You can marry an African. You can marry a Russian. You can even marry an American. But – by God – be sure to check with me first, before you bring home a Belgian".'

Aside from the publishing operation and weekly visits from authors and diplomats, Dick is not completely alone in the house at 328 Church Street. Besides me, there is another 'PG' (paying guest, our host insists on the nomenclature), a man four years younger than Dick, but disabled by a desert climbing accident 30 years before. Had it not been for a timely airlift out of the Persian Gulf, and a pioneering surgeon in London, Roddy would have lost his right leg; instead, he walks with a limp and is bothered by aches in cold weather (which he never mentions; he merely winces). He doesn't discuss the incident – indeed I never encountered a person less self-pitying than him.

'Easy come, easy go,' was his favourite phrase, a philosophy that served him well in a life of near-constant movement, and from what I gathered, his final years living with Dick were, perhaps, the most settled of his life. Dick would joke, 'My *poor* brother, he's so misguided. He thinks that Roddy and I are *gay*.' I'm not sure whether anyone who knew them intimately would have imagined that. 'I don't know about you, Roddy,' Dick would say, hungrily eyeing a beef fillet in the kitchen, 'but after I've eaten a rare steak, I need a – a *really good* woman.' The younger man would give a grunt of amusement whenever Dick said something he agreed with, rolling his eyes when his friend went too far.

Eric Lionel Roderick 'Roddy' Jones was born in Palestine in 1934. Returning to Britain aged ten, he was old enough to know the difference between Haifa and Glasgow, and as soon as he was able, he moved back to the Middle East. His perfect Arabic, learned as a major in the Royal Welsh Fusiliers, and his humble discretion, earned him several important advisory roles in distant corners of the Arabian Peninsula. In the decades following his retirement from the army, he worked for two successive Sultans of Oman. Part dirty British coaster, part quinquireme of Nineveh, he combined physical delicacy and robustness within a compact, handsome frame.

Years of cold-water swimming in the Serpentine and the Euphrates had accentuated his broad shoulders with the result that, at not much over five foot two, his sturdy torso appeared far wider than it was in reality. His hair was completely white, as were his Jupiter-like brows. It blew about his schoolboy ears in the wind but was more usually combed back high over his forehead or covered by a *pakool*, an Afghan beret; he was fastidious about his appearance. His nose was delicate, almost feminine. His determined lips opened only when absolutely necessary, lending him an air of mystery that Dick denied he possessed. Happy to remain completely taciturn, he never gave way to flights of fancy – except where women were concerned.

He first came to live with Dick at the turn of the new millennium, after his second wife found him guilty of a one-sided, and purely epistolary, love affair. When she succumbed to cancer six months later, Roddy left Church Street to nurse her through the final stages of her illness. Refusing an offer of staying on in the marital home after her death, he returned to Kensington and resumed his place as the happy shadow of his boon companion and patron. He loved to talk about Dick's kindness, how morning or night he would, without hesitation, open his door to friends or strangers with the same smile, the same easy grace. But he never took this generosity for granted. 'All Dick has to do is ask me to "bugger off",' Roddy confided in me a few months before he died, and I knew he meant what he said. With unquestioning gratitude, he would have got up and left. His passions were obscure and subtle.

When I first get to know Dick's wife, Susan, an artist, her memory and words are beginning to crack with the onset of Alzheimer's disease. Willowy and statuesque – in photographs of the couple in the early years of their marriage she looks almost as tall as Dick – the young woman was presented at court soon after the end of the war, and that whole season smote the young men with her charm (abundant), wit (acerbic) and vice-like grip (as a dance partner). She was always good with her hands.

Because of her memory problems, I often find it easier to talk to Susan about her sculptures and paintings, solid objects we can touch and describe together. One day, standing in her gallery at sunset, our words are interrupted by a passing bus that sets the sculptures reverberating: a giant pair of brazen legs coiled one about the other; an artist's left hand, bronze knuckles gleaming, finger joints poised for action; the marble relief of a tiny newborn, poignant in its round rump and chubby arms, more grave stele than birthday souvenir. It is a sombre thought. Nodding towards the baby's bottom, I try to revive the light-hearted tone of our broken exchange.

'So, how many children do you have?'

'Oh, lots. Four – no – maybe five, I think.'

I smiled at what I thought was a wry sense of humour.

'Did they all grow up here?'

'Oh, no, some of them were born in the country.'

'Ah, yes, I heard that you used to live in East Sussex. Isn't that where you learned to sculpt?'

I had heard the story, of course, from Dick. Driving to a friend's house for dinner one evening, they nearly came off the road when their tyre-rim struck part of a felled tree. They had stopped the engine in order to move it, but Susan insisted they take it with them, and had spent all night carving the oak into the likeness of her husband – to the mixed delight and chagrin of their hosts. I remember reading somewhere that excessive insularity can be a precursor of the disease that would later take hold of her brain, robbing her of everything but the most elemental of memories; I thought of her retreating into herself in a corner of the dining room, barely touching a morsel of food, drinking only water, and singularly digging away at that dead wood, while her hands recreated her consort's commanding brow and sensuous lips.

'Oh, no. I learned my trade in London.'

'But five children, though,' I grinned, 'that's a lot! You must have been very young when you had them. And working too. I can't imagine having children now.' I was twenty-five.

'No, you'll see, they give you a huge amount of pleasure.'

'It must be very rewarding.'

'Oh, yes, it is. And when you've created them yourself—'

'What an achievement!'

'But, of course, I've always been good with my hands.'

'What?'

'Yes, to make something with your hands, to create, that is the most important thing anyone can do.'

'I suppose you are right...'

Later, when she could neither talk to me about her children, her marriage or her art, I mourned the loss of her memories on her behalf.

For most of the first two years that I lived in the house, Dick had a weekly ritual: to clean the street-level windows of a compound of half-ingested broccoli, brown bread and grape pips (or variations thereof). He never understood what caused it. 'Fucking seagulls,' he'd say, grabbing, to my horror, a kitchen sponge or a tea towel and setting to work on the ancient, dirty panes that coyly observed the pavement of Church Street.

I didn't think much of his theory about seagulls.

Dick would enthuse about how he'd persuaded Dulwich College to sell him the freehold in 1982. For him, the house is its own entity and the effort he went through to pay for it is comparable to the pain his wife went through to produce five children. Sometimes I wonder if the house isn't his sixth.

The house was falling apart when Dick got the lease of the place in 1969. For several years, the family stayed on in Sussex while he tried to make it habitable. It was 'primitive,' according to Dick, and not very nice to look at from the outside. Did they ever have lodgers? I asked him recently. He thought for a bit, remembering suddenly with a smile. 'Yes! We inherited one. There was a woman upstairs. She was writing an *interminable* book...' The stream of paying guests continued; one of his daughters told me, 'Dad was always filling the house with people, for ages I didn't have a proper bedroom because Dad rented mine out, I lived in the basement which was full of coal.' But there were also treasures underground.

'The cellar was full of sculptures by Jacob Epstein,' Dick tells a lunch party early on in my tenure. The leaseholders before him were the economist Wynne Godley and his wife Kitty Epstein, daughter of Jacob, and first wife of Lucian Freud. Society biographies, almost incredulously, gush about the beautiful home Kitty curated at the start of her second marriage – as if any woman who'd been dumped by Freud (in truth she walked out, exasperated) would be too traumatised to do anything as strenuous as put flowers in glass jars or organise parties. Yet the house does have a healing atmosphere, in the quality of light that filters in through the garden doors, echoing the soothing green of the same William Morris wallpaper that Kitty's friends remarked upon.

Lucian Freud bought the house five doors away a decade later and, it would seem, despite the passing of years, hadn't managed to forgive his first wife for leaving him. A couple of months before the artist's death Dick received a telephone call from his neighbour. 'Dick, I want to speak to you about Lucian, I think he's gone mad. I saw him gobbing at your windows yesterday.' The neighbour suggested an explanation for Freud's behaviour, which had been going on for decades unnoticed, but only recently become so flagrant that passers-by had remarked on it: he had never recovered from the shock of losing Kitty, and in the absence of a voodoo doll had been avenging himself on the house ever since.

NOTE – Certain names and locations have been changed, to protect the privacy of living persons.

FRANCES LORD

Frances Lord is a writer and curator with a background in the visual arts, with particular specialism in contemporary craft and commissioning projects for the public realm. She has worked for the Crafts Council, as Director of a Sculpture Trust and as a freelance on a variety of arts and cultural projects.

franceslord@btinternet.com
www.franceslord.com

Gossip as fresh as yesterday

Gossip as fresh as yesterday is an extract from a wider research project set in Cornwall and London which explores the life and work of her father, the artist David Haughton.

David Haughton, *View of St Just*, 1950s, oil on canvas, 55 x 101 cm
Photo © Jonathan Bassett

David Haughton was a talented, independent-minded twenty-three year old when he first came to Cornwall in 1947. He had dropped out of the Slade a few years earlier, dissatisfied with what he viewed as its inadequacies:

> 'What I wanted from an art school was contact with older painters who understood you. Somebody you could go out and have a beer with, talk to naturally. All the staff at that time were elderly, so remote, and didn't come anywhere near the students if they could help it. I needed a connection with the arts as a personal, social thing, as well as simply learning mechanically how to draw, which I didn't find at the Slade, so I left.'[1]

---

1 *David Haughton: Back to St Just*, transcript of an unpublished interview between DH and Stephen Prince, 5th August 1980, Central School of Art Library Archive.

David was drawn not to picturesque St Ives where the modernist artists Ben Nicholson, Barbara Hepworth and Russian émigré Naum Gabo had moved in 1939 to escape war-torn London, and where Cornish-born abstract painter Peter Lanyon lived, but to the windswept moors of West Cornwall. David did not hold much truck with St Ives, describing it as 'a very pretty town best seen from the railway... an enchanting hallucination with its narrow streets and cobbled courtyards.'[2] Despite these attractions there was, in his opinion, 'a whiff of corruption in the air, like so many low-lying towns surrounded by steep hills. That and a lively tourist trade, a dying fishing industry, and artists, with their paranoia and general provincialism, you can gather it's not my favourite place.'[3]

Instead David and his girlfriend, Lali Fenyves, moved into Croftpool, a remote cottage near Nancledra owned by a local farmer, paying five shillings a week rent. The couple had met as art students in London, while David was at the Slade and Lali at the Chelsea School of Art. David had written to his old Slade friend, Bryan Wynter, who would become one of the best known artists of his generation, to ask if he knew of anywhere they could rent. Wynter proposed Croftpool, 'an absolute gem of a cottage,' on the moors between Zennor and The Carn in the hamlet of Morvah, where Bryan and his wife Monica lived. The prospect of post-war cheap living was an attractive proposition for young London-based, Soho drinking artists and writers who gravitated south-west towards the land of ancient myth, quoits and the famed quality of light. Some, such as the poet W S Graham and artists Patrick Heron, Terry Frost and Roger and Rose Hilton, permanently settled in the area.

The writer Ilse Barker and her artist husband Kit lived twenty minutes' walk away at an equally remote cottage, Noon Veor, near Zennor, and often stayed at Croftpool overnight. Ilse later recalled:

> 'There was a bus from Penzance followed by what seemed to me a very long walk through farmland and over moors. I thought their cottage very romantic. There were few amenities. Water had to be fetched from a nearby stream, there was a privy round the back, cooking was done on primus and paraffin stoves, and one went to bed with a candle. David always had several paintings going, so the living room was full of the paraphernalia

2 DH writing in the early 1980s; author's archive.
3 ibid.

of paintings; canvases leaned against the walls, and a lovely smell of oil paint mixed with the cooking smells.'[4]

Lali, in between catching the bus into St Ives to do waitressing work, was the model for his early portraits. In some she sits quietly, in repose, with folded hands, on the ubiquitous artist's Windsor chair set against a background of Wyndham Lewis-influenced vivid strips of red, green, blue and yellow. In others an elaborately folded length of fabric is balanced on her head, or she is depicted foregrounded, in the manner of a still life, with the dramatic contours of the moors behind. Constantly drawing, David captured Lali and the surrounding landscape, gradually evolving and developing his own style.

David chose his muse well. On Ilse Barker's first meeting with Lali and David in a tearoom in nearby Penzance, she was 'stunned by Lali's beauty,' and her 'long black hair and fine oval face with very dark eyes.' David she described as 'small and slight,' 'intelligent and lively.'[5]

Lali, 1949 Mixed Media, 28.5 x 33 cm
Photo © Jonathan Bassett

4 Talbot, Katherine (Ilse Barker's writing name), *Kit Barker Cornwall 1947-1948 Recollections of Painters and Writers*, St Ives: The Book Gallery, 1993, p7.
5 ibid, p7.

Ilse later learnt that Lali was herself art school-trained and, when pressed, admitted 'to doing the occasional drawing.'[6] Lali and David's domestic arrangement was not at all unusual at that time – the creative talents of girlfriends and wives often lying dormant while they financially, domestically and emotionally supported their male partners' careers.

Another glimpse into David and Lali's life at Croftpool comes from a series of wonderfully evocative letters written by David to their great friend, the painter and printmaker Prunella Clough, in the late 1940s. Rediscovering the letters in the 1990s at the back of her plan chest, Prunella was reminded of 'the art of letter writing,' and 'the evocation of Cornwall and gossip fresh as yesterday.'[7] Written in a clear, legible script, sometimes over a period of weeks, the letters are indeed a marvellous read, evoking the creative and financial challenges of these formative years in West Cornwall.

David was a hard worker and disciplined; most days he would set off to walk and fill a sketchbook with drawings of the moors, later vividly describing what he saw in his letters. He notes the annual ritual of burning the gorse, with 'the black earth and ochre and green (bright viridian!) grass' contrasting against a blue sky and 'the wonderful smoke rising up like a fan.' Returning to the makeshift studio at Croftpool he would work on oil sketches, having prepared 'a great array of small boards and panels.'[8] His observations and delight in the seasonal changes of colour and texture fed back into his work. Conversational in tone, these letters move between vivid descriptions of the West Penwith landscape, the petty squabbles and professional and personal rivalries taking place in nearby St Ives, and his dealings with London buyers and galleries. The late 1940s was a significant time in establishing St Ives as a centre of internationally recognised modern art. Artistic bickering and concerns about 'mediocrity' surfaced when Nicholson, Hepworth, Peter Lanyon and the potter Bernard Leach broke away from the 'traditionalists' (or in David's words the 'archaic craftsmen and pretty view painters') to form a new exhibiting group, the *Penwith Society of Arts* – still going today.

Prunella Clough, five years older and already recognised for her portrayal of industrial scenes and the detritus of urban and rural living, was one of David's acknowledged artistic influences at that time. David itched to paint greenhouses and cold frames, initially wary of appropriating two of Prunella's favourite subjects. Eventually he gave in, arguing, 'What the

---

6 Ibid, p7.
7 Prunella Clough letter to Lali Broido (née Fenyves), 7 December 1995, author's archive.
8 DH letter to PC, 1947, author's archive.

hell, P Clough is not the only one allowed to paint greenhouses.'[9] His depictions of this subject, formal explorations of 'the transparencies of white and grey and alternate umber and white stripes,'[10] sold at *The Third Annual Crypt Exhibition* in St Ives in 1948 and later in the inaugural exhibition of the *Penwith Society of Arts* in St Ives in 1949.

The post-war shortage of materials and cash was a constant lament. Prunella, as ever, came to the rescue. Responding to an exasperated mention of a 'ridiculous shortage of Flake White and Viridian… unobtainable down here – there being only one art shop and a million painters using a quite unnecessary amount of the stuff,'[11] Prunella posted sufficient quantities to save the day and enable an exhibition deadline to be met.

As well as dispatching paints and other supplies, Prunella acted as part mentor/part informal London agent, organising the urgent couriering of picture frames down to Cornwall, collecting unsold paintings from exhibitions and storing these at her house or posting them on to Croftpool. In addition to these acts of kindness, generous gifts of wine appeared at Christmas and the occasional postal order helped nourish body and soul. In return Prunella would receive newsy, gossipy letters, and frequent and pressing invitations to stay at Croftpool for a break: 'I know it wouldn't be a waste of time – bring your paints – I've quite a few little boards that I could spare – if you'd like to use them.'[12]

Despite the charm and inspiration of the Cornish landscape, the pull of the London art scene remains ever-present: from the desire to see 'some originals' in the Tate's big Van Gogh exhibition of 1947, to the importance of maintaining an artistic presence in the city. While preparing new work to show at Browse & Delbanco's summer show and Gimpel Fils in Cork Street, David ponders whether to sell a landscape to 'an enormous woman who lives in a tiny cottage at a reduced price of £12 [to be paid] by instalments of £1 a week.'[13] This was all happening at the same time as he and Lali were given notice to quit Croftpool to make way for the farmer's newly-married son and the 'impossibility of finding another vacant affordable cottage nearby.' The promise of a teaching job in Falmouth – 'teach for three hours a day and then your own time. It's the sort of thing I would find very stimulating'[14] – did not materialise, necessitating a spot of modelling

9   DH letter to PC, undated, author's archive.
10 Ibid.
11 DH letter to PC, 1947.
12 Ibid.
13 DH letter to PC, 1949.
14 Ibid.

('an awful job') to scrape together some extra money.¹⁵

London social connections were also maintained. Friends would visit, many of whom would later become well-known artists and writers. There was the week David spent drawing on the Scilly Isles with fellow artist Kit Barker and 'a young German poet Michael Hamburger.' There are several references to The Two Roberts – Robert MacBryde and Robert Colquhoun – firm friends since his Slade days, despite the fact that David was, in his words, 'neither Scottish nor homosexual.'¹⁶ Irritation surfaces in the Prunella letters as David vents his frustration at not being able to 'work a little faster.' How he envies 'the Roberts, MacBryde especially, who just sprouts paintings in between cooking, sweeping and renunciations of the English – he's a marvel.'¹⁷

Unable to find another cottage to rent and 'sick of being poor,' David and Lali returned to London to seek work. In 1951, bolstered by references from the art critic Herbert Read and Ben Nicholson, David was appointed part-time painting lecturer at the Central School of Art and Design, where he taught for the next thirty years.

However, the pull of the Cornish landscape, and the artistic response it inspired, never disappeared. David would return repeatedly, staying in the former tin mining village of St Just-in-Penwith, ten miles north of Land's End. Here, in this most westerly town in the British Isles, he would draw the grey granite buildings, the Wesleyan chapel, the deserted back streets, and the derelict tin mine chimneys and engine houses set deep into the rugged landscape. Back in his London studio the drawings were worked up into intricately detailed etchings and oil paintings.

The years 1947–50 spent at Croftpool were formative. David's meticulous observation and recording of the scarred mining landscape and ancient bracken and gorse moorland continued to offer him artistic and spiritual nourishment for the rest of his working life.

Recalling this period in the 1980s, he described his experience of discovering St Just, the town that became for him a microcosm of the whole of Cornwall, and a feeling of travelling back in time:

15 Ibid.
16 Bristow, Roger *The Last Bohemians The Two Roberts – Colquhoun & MacBryde*, Edinburgh: Samson & Co, 2010, p 131.
17 DH letter to PC, 1949.

'The cottages all had a slightly forlorn look, rather like old sepia photographs, old and defaced. I was only twenty-three or four... but as I came down the hill I suddenly had what, for want of a better word, was a mystical experience. I don't know exactly what happened to me, but I do know that it was the single most important event of my life... the whole world seemed to be a living presence. I have often thought about it, wondering if it was truly a manifestation of a divine nature, a transcendental visitation, or merely a product of my own rather exulted frame of mind. But I do know that it was utterly beautiful and in fact a day does not pass, when in some way I am reminded of it, specially when I am working, it changed my life on that spring day.'[18]

St Just Square and Church postcard: DH archive

18 DH, writing in the early 1980s, author's archive.

YIRU PENG

Yiru Peng has spent half her life in Singapore and half in China. Her work focuses on contemporary issues in the mainland, where personal encounters with education, censorship, the internet, history, and language all intersect in her search for what it means to come of age in present-day China.

pengyiru1222@gmail.com

On Floor Nine
An extract

My favourite place on the ninth floor is the restroom. To be exact, the last stall down the left, closest to the tinted windows. We are approximately one and a half blocks away from one of the fanciest shopping districts in town, and from this particular window, you can admire the monochromatic succession of distant storefronts: grey-black, white, and then ivory. Prada, Chanel, and Louis Vuitton. In front of their gilded doors, cars trickle up and down the road, the glare of their hoods muffled to a pleasing glimmer by the dust and grime on the windows.

I am currently working here as a summer intern. The company I work for – a chain of tuition facilities that specialise in teaching English – owns three floors in our building: floors eight, nine, and twenty-four. I have been to the twenty-fourth floor only once (on the excuse of borrowing their printer when ours had choked on a sheet of paper), and the view from their toilet was even more spectacular.

Within this glossy downtown office building we are not the sole enterprise invested in international education and general hothousing. Floors eleven and twelve belong to a company that targets middle school students and their parents, offering extracurricular tuition in Maths, Science, Chinese, and English. Floor thirteen belongs to a centre that teaches Japanese and Korean. Floor fifteen is quartered by three companies that teach Spanish, German, and French respectively; and one exam centre – SIELE, or Servicio Internacional de Evaluación de la Lengua Española – a formal exam that proves and legitimises your proficiency in Spanish.

To cap it all off, floor twenty-five, the top floor in the building, is home to an immigration company that aims to assist Chinese nationals in obtaining foreign visas.

On some mornings when I arrive during peak hours, untimely enough to get crushed at the back of the lift, I have to wait until the lift goes all the way up and starts descending again before I can alight at my floor. On these days, it is intriguing to see what awaits me behind the smooth chrome doors. Sometimes it is just the boring, understated lettering of a stock exchange or an insurance agency, but sometimes they slide open and reveal a barrage of colorful advertisements. The bold block prints pounce on you immediately: Do you dream of travelling to Europe? Japan? Korea? Do you wish to study and live abroad? Come learn with us and earn your certificate within six months! All this is set on half-transparent, overly saturated prints of the Eiffel tower, or Mount Fuji, or Cologne Cathedral.

In comparison, the advertisement banners on our floor are much less exotic: just blow-up lists of redacted student names and their scores. To have your asterisked name make it to this glorified list, you simply have to score above 100 in the TOEFL. But then again, the acronym alone is advertisement enough – as one of the most widely accepted English language proficiency tests in the world, and the gatekeeper to any English-speaking academic institution (as well as several that aren't), almost every non-Anglophone international student has heard of it. Ironic, since the majority of the Anglophone world may go through their whole lives blissfully oblivious of its existence.

In a word, this is the crux of my job here as a part-time teaching assistant – to help students score better on English language tests.

I am nearly one month into the job now and coping surprisingly well. Yanhui and I have grown amicable enough for me jokingly to vent my exasperation at her abysmal memorising skills and for her not to take it personally. Her mom had finally caved in and fell for the deluxe study package – Yanhui's schedule is now booked fully from one end of the week to the other with reading, listening, speaking, and writing classes. I now have the pleasure of reading through her utterly incomprehensible compositions and trying to help her transform them into readable English before Yanhui hands them in to her writing teacher.

I, of course, make full use of our new-found familiarity to express my incredulousness at the quality of her writing.

'What are you even trying to express here? I can't make head nor tail of this sentence; it doesn't even make sense in Chinese.'

'Umm...' Yanhui squints at the passage. 'I think I was trying to say, "scientific evidence proves that the ancient bees' nests also had waterproof structures."'

'Well then, you have to spell it out. You can't just mash a bunch of key words together and hope they'll come out as an English sentence.'

Yanhui groans and flops down on her desk. 'Ugggh. I hate English.'

I circle another misspelled word with my red pen. 'Why do you even need a TOEFL score anyway? I thought you were going to Japan.'

Yanhui props her chin on one arm. 'Well, I'm applying as an international student. Having a good TOEFL score gives me an edge. Besides, lots of first year courses for international students are taught in English.'

'Huh. Sounds complicated.' Yanhui nods in agreement. 'Then why even go to Japan in the first place? If you went anywhere else, you wouldn't have to learn two languages at once.'

'Well, my mom owns a company that does Kadō. You know, Japanese floral design? She flies to Japan half a dozen times a year.'

This is the first I've heard her say so much about herself. 'And that's, like, the single reason why you have to go to Japan?'

'Well... that and the fact that I didn't do so well in the college entrance exam.' Yanhui makes a face. 'I guess now that we know each other it doesn't matter if I tell you – my parents are divorced. I lived with my dad throughout high school, and he was so strict with me I basically had a depressive breakdown. I only started living with my mom last year. She doesn't really force me to do anything, and I probably have a better chance of getting into a good school in Japan than I do here, so,' Yanhui shrugs. 'It's not like I mind having to go to Japan.'

For the first time, I get the feeling that I've been too quick to judge. 'Well,' I begin awkwardly, trying to gauge how much I should share in exchange for such a personal piece of information. 'My parents are both university professors. My dad's been bugging me all through senior year to apply for a PhD, even though I told him I'd rather jump in front of a train than have to spend another five years of my life studying.'

Yanhui laughs at that. 'I guess parents are just all the same.'

Sometime in August, Ms Chen quits her job. More likely leaping into the arms of one of our rival companies, where she can get a few per cent more on her monthly commission for her six-figure sales. There's no lack of demand in this industry for someone with a glib tongue.

Before she left, I did get a chance to see her in action, once, when I was manning the reception desk in the lounge. A middle-aged woman wearing a styled, mid-length bob, with sunglasses perched on top of her head and a massive Coach handbag swinging from her elbow, came in and asked for Ms Chen. She was evidently a parent of one of our students, so I dutifully went into the office to fetch my supervisor.

'Mrs Fang, it's so nice to see you again! Please, please, sit.'

Having done my job, I slunk back behind the receptionist desk. The two women struck up a friendly conversation, and within a few minutes it was obvious that Mrs Fang was very fond of Ms Chen. For all her superiority towards her subordinates, Ms Chen was very skilled in the art of saying the right thing at the right time to the right person. The conversation veered naturally from Mrs Fang's new haircut to her daughter, Jiamin. I recalled having given her dictation a few times – she was one of my 'favourites', meaning dictation with her was practically a breeze.

'Jiamin is doing very well in her lessons. It's not challenging for her, really – she has a remarkably good foundation. Has she decided yet whether she wants to do the IB or the AP programme?'

'No, but I've been talking to her friends' parents and it seems that one way or the other we will have to send her to Shanghai.'

'Of course,' Ms Chen agreed readily. 'All the best international schools are in Shanghai.'

Mrs Fang sighed dramatically. 'I'm just worried she might not be able to adapt so quickly. And she changes her mind so often! Just last week she told me she doesn't want to major in biology any more, she's taken an interest in linguistics!'

'It's perfectly natural of course, for children her age,' Ms Chen appeased. 'If anything, it's a good thing – we have so many students here who can barely make up their own mind about anything.'

'Yes, in a way, I'm also relieved.' Mrs Fang sounded pleased. 'She isn't afraid to try out new things. And each time we give her our full support – it is always important for us parents to support our children's interests,' Mrs Fang said sagely.

'Yes, indeed.' Mrs Chen nodded along. 'I'm so glad you and Mr Fang are so liberal in your education. Jiamin is very special – she's always so happy-go-lucky and full of enthusiasm about everything.'

'Exactly! Some parents are just so strict and controlling, you know? I've never seen the point in it, you raise a child like that for what? fifteen years? and then they become depressed and commit suicide. We've almost never been strict with Jiamin, and she turned out so well,' Mrs Fang announced proudly.

'You've gotten really lucky with a daughter like Jiamin. Of course –' Ms Chen caught herself just in time, '– it must have a lot to do with the way you brought her up.'

Ms Fang was about to reply when Jiamin came out of her classroom. Class had just been dismissed. She gave a look of surprise when she saw her mother sitting in the lobby.

'What are you doing here?' Jiamin asked, eyeing her mom suspiciously.

'I was just talking to Ms Chen about your studies.' Mrs Fang stretched out a hand and Jiamin approached reluctantly, evidently embarrassed at such a blatant act of affection in a public space.

'What's there to talk about?' Jiamin groused. 'In any case, I can't talk right now, I need to go to the toilet. Class starts again in ten minutes.'

'It's fine, run along now,' Ms Chen assured her. 'We'll have plenty of time to talk again later.'

A few weeks later, I was back in the study room, unpacking my takeout. It was lunch hour, and the room was mostly vacant, everyone having left for lunch. I took a seat in the back row, closest to the door, hoping that the smell of food would waft away faster here, or I would be stuck with it for the next five hours. I was just breaking apart my chopsticks when Jiamin and her friend entered the room, their hands full of takeout and bubble tea.

The two girls took a seat in the first row. Amid the rustle of plastic bags being crumpled and the screech of straws piercing drink caps, I heard Jiamin complain to her friend: 'I'm just so sick and tired of it.'

'Of what?' her friend asked.

'My mom,' Jiamin replied. 'One of these days she's gonna make me want to jump off a roof.'

HENRY REICHARD

Henry Reichard grew up on a sheep farm in rural Maryland. He studied mathematics and physics at Yale, then spent a year writing in Chile before coming to UEA. He writes creative non-fiction and speculative fiction, often about nature or mathematics. He's also an avid long-distance runner.
hal.reichard@gmail.com

Birth

An excerpt from a longer piece, told from the perspective of a new-born lamb, about life on a sheep farm. It is part of a collection of animal vignettes set on the farm.

EARLY SUMMER

The world's beating heart hangs high above me. It's a bright-white circle that swims slowly across the wide-open-blue and, as it moves, warmth swells out of it the same way warmth used to swell out of mother's heart when I was still within her, and all the short-straight-greens and the tall-crooked-browns turn to it and rest within its warmth the same way that I used to rest within mother's. I can't bear to look at the bright-white, but I always know it's there because the world wakes up when it comes near.

I'm not afraid anymore. I don't want to go back to the darkness.

I'm bigger now. The bright-white has gone up and come down many times. Mother won't let me drink from her anymore. For a while I was so hungry that I thought I would go back to the darkness even though I didn't want to. But then mother showed me how to eat the short-straight-green and the three-leaf-narrow-stem, and she taught me not to eat the prickly-stem-blood-in-mouth or the wide-leaf-burning-tongue. Then she showed me how to hide under the tall-crooked-brown when the bright-white is making me hot, and she brought me to the place where the clear-moving-cold lies between the tall-crooked-browns, and there were others like me there, and we played with each other and splashed in the clear-moving-cold. Now I play with the others every time the bright-white comes up in the sky. I'm almost never hungry.

There are so many of us. Sometimes I still can't believe how many we are. Now I see that there are others, that there is a world beyond mother, a bright-white shining in the wide-open-blue – another beating heart stronger than hers. And mother is no longer everything, she is no longer a She, no longer the world – and I see that there is reason to live in this new world, even though I will never again be as close to her as I once was, when I lived in the world within her. Every time the bright-white rises I run out with the others over the hills covered by the short-straight-green. I baa to short-legs-long-ears, and she baas back to me. Sometimes curling-wool-caught-in-branches runs over and baas fiercely, and then the three of us race each other over the wide-rolling-green towards the huge-square-distant-brown where the two-legs live. When we start getting too far away, mother always baas to me. *Bãååâ bãââã?* she asks, and *báaœā báaœā!* I reply. But sometimes she says *baäà baäà baäà!* And then I have to go back to her, and she takes me to the warm-square-close-brown, and we hide from the wolves.

The wolves are black and white and have long, cruel mouths with long, sharp teeth. I thought they were friends at first, and I went up to touch noses with one of them. But mother cried out *baœåœ! baœåœ! baœåœ!* and ran between me and the wolf, and the wolf snarled and showed its long fangs to mother, and then I knew it wasn't a friend. Mother is afraid of the wolves, even though they're smaller than her. All of us are scared of the wolves.

But the two-legs aren't. The two-legs are friends with the wolves. The wolves live with the two-legs and follow them around, and if the two-legs want to they can make the wolves come to them and do what they want. Mother says it's because the two-legs feed lambs-that-haven't-obeyed-their-mothers to the wolves – she says that's why the wolves obey the two-legs. But I don't believe her. The wolves must eat the short-straight-green like we do. Except their teeth are so long and thin I don't know how they chew it.

There's one two-leg that's different from the others. She's short for a two-leg, and most days she's brown, but some days she's black and white like the wolves or red like a bird or white like us. The wolves are friends with all the two-legs, but they're more than friends with her. They follow her around as if they were lambs and she were their mother. As if she were their bright-white in the wide-open-blue. I call her mother-of-wolves. Some days she comes out and brings one of the wolves into the wide-rolling-green with us, and all the other wolves howl together in the huge-square-distant-brown. She makes high shrill sounds like bird calls, then the wolf runs out around us, moving closer or farther away as she calls to it, and we run away from the wolf into new wide-rolling-greens, and after we've gone into them, mother-of-wolves shuts the long-brown-trapping behind us so we can't get out again.

And afterwards mother is always scared, and she tells me that the two-legs are as bad as the wolves, and that mother-of-wolves is the worst of all. But I don't believe her, because when I think back to the first day when I came out of the darkness, I remember the first two-leg I saw, the one that lifted me up when I couldn't stand on my own, and that two-leg was mother-of-wolves. And mother-of-wolves was the one who gave short-straight-golden-dry to mother when it was so cold that there wasn't anything else to eat, and mother would have gone back to the darkness without the short-straight-golden-dry, and I would have gone with her, and mother-of-wolves was also the one who helped curling-wool-caught-in-branches on the day when he was trapped in the tall-crooked-browns.

And so I don't think mother-of-wolves is as bad as the wolves, even if she's friends with them. She cares for us. I think she's also mother-of-sheep.

LATE SUMMER

i am one of many. i am part of Us.

Before, i was part of an us of only two – an us of just me and mother. But now i am part of an Us that spreads across the entire world. An Us that baas always to itself, from the time the bright-white rises into the wide-open-blue until the time it sinks into the flat-far-away-brown. An Us that warms itself in the cold and the darkness, that looks after the ones who are weak or hurt. An Us that protects me, guides me, shows me the way to the short-straight-green and circles around me when the wolves come.

i am held within Us the same way i was once held within mother. And now i see that i am not alone, that i have never been alone, because i have always been a part of Us, only until now i was caught within myself – i was caught within myself like curling-wool-caught-in-branches on the day when he was caught in the tall-crooked-browns, or else i was blind like wanders-too-close-to-wolves, who cannot see a tall-crooked-brown or a patch of short-straight-green or even a wolf until her nose is nearly touching it. i was as blind as her, maybe even more blind, because i thought i was alone when i was always surrounded by Us – when Us was already calling out to me, calling *Welcome! Welcome!* as soon as i came out of the darkness.

Mother does not watch me so closely anymore. i wander far away from her, wander close to the long-brown-trapping and the many-tall-crooked-browns. Mother trusts Us to watch after me. When the bright-white rises into the wide-open-blue i rise with it, and soon after, when Us begins baaing to itself, i remember that i am a part of Us, and i recognise my own voice and mother's voice in the baaing of Us, and i am happy. The world is covered with the short-straight-green, with so many short-straight-greens that no one could count them, but together they make a single never-ending-green that covers the entire world. i am like a single short-straight-green that anyone might eat on any day. But i am part of an Us, and that Us is the never-ending-green that covers the world.

    We are far away from the wolves now. We are in a place beyond the clear-moving-cold, where the short-straight-green is longer than it was before, where the three-leaf-narrow-stem is everywhere. We are safe here. We are always eating, and the younger of Us grow larger every day. The older ones grow fatter. Some days the little-two-legs come down from the huge-square-distant-brown and play in the clear-moving-cold, as We used to. Or else they walk unsteadily under the tall-crooked-browns, and We baa to each other and watch them and wonder how they balance on just two legs.

    And so Our days pass. We grow larger and fatter. The bright-white shines above Us. In the long time between the rising and falling of the bright-white, We eat and wander and rest beneath the tall-crooked-browns, and in the times of resting the older ones speak to the younger ones and tell them of what We remember. We remember the time when one of the wolves – a red one, not black like the others – came down and bit one of Us and dragged her away, baaing, bleating, screaming – dragged her and bit her until she turned red and stopped struggling and stopped bleating. And afterwards mother-of-wolves came with her mate, angrier than We had ever seen her, shouting at the wolf who had taken one of Us, and her mate grabbed the red wolf and had to drag him away, because he did not obey the two-legs as the other wolves did, and mother-of-wolves sat down beside the one of Us that had been bitten and put her hands on the places where Our wool was red and cried. The red wolf was still howling even as the mate of mother-of-wolves dragged him away. He is still with them now, living in the huge-square-distant-brown, waiting for his chance to drag away another of Us.

    The young ones listen to these memories wide-eyed. We had not believed there were such terrible things in the world. We have seen the wolves, yes, but the younger among Us have never seen them bite and drag one of Us away. The wolves we know all obey mother-of-wolves. And mother-of-wolves is Our friend.

    You believe that? the older ones ask. *You really believe that?*

    Why shouldn't we?

    And then there is a difference between Us, a separation between old and young. Because the old ones will not explain what they mean. We come to see that there is a little us contained within Us – the little us of little ones, young ones, who do not understand what We mean, who perhaps never will. And it is Us that is strong, Us that will survive, as the never-ending-green survives, no matter how many short-straight-greens are eaten. But what of us?

What frightens us most is diminishing, dwindling, until all that remains is the lonely i from which we all escaped, to which none of us wants to return. To be an i again – alone, separated from us and from Us. The thought is more terrible than the stories about the red wolf. We ask our mothers to explain about mother-of-wolves, but they shake their heads and turn back to the short-straight-green.

They tell us to eat well.

They tell us to grow fat and lazy and to take happiness in Us and in Our time under the bright-white.

They tell us that we will not be able to do these things much longer.

And so our days pass, and we continue eating and growing larger and fatter, but all the while a fear spreads among us. We wonder about the cold-yet-to-come. And about the other thing, the thing the old ones said to us. We wonder whether mother-of-wolves is really our friend.

JANNITA SMITH

Jannita Smith worked as an actor, acrobat, human cannonball, and copywriter before embarking on a teaching career. For the last eight years, she has taught in an international school in Hong Kong, been creative director of the performance group *Hong Kong Stories* and made regular appearances as a stand-up comedian.

jannita.smith@icloud.com

Fit For What?
An excerpt

Seventy sweaty bodies slither their way across the floor. Opposing arms and legs stretch out in unison accompanied by intermittent groans. Suddenly, they hit reverse, limbs retract and extend backwards sending a giant ripple of movement to the opposite wall. These are not alien invaders from the latest science fiction or some cutting-edge robot experiment, but real human beings – pretending to be geckos.

According to the new 'man-bun brigade' of personal trainers it is a functional exercise which means it not only loads the muscles but forces the brain to work extra hard in co-ordinating movement. And I can confirm that this is true, as I am one of the seventy participants sprawled across the floor desperately trying to keep my belly up and make some new, neurological connections.

It is a Saturday afternoon on the outskirts of Vienna, a sleepy suburb where the city tram reaches the end of the line. Nestled next to woodland is a community sports hall where sixty-three men and seven women have arrived from all over Europe, and a few beyond, to work with the latest fitness training guru, Ido Portal.

Though not a household name, Portal is influencing fitness fanatics across the globe. His philosophy of 'movement culture' has permeated gyms and added to the multi-billion dollar health and fitness industry that is growing all around the world. He is, perhaps, best known for teaching movement skills to Irish Mixed Martial Arts (MMA) World Champion, Conor McGregor, for his fight against World Champion American boxer Floyd Mayweather – a bout that made several hundred million dollars and lasted under thirty minutes.

There are no world champions in the old sports hall in Vienna. At least it doesn't look that way. This is an eclectic mix of young and old, toned and gangly. Half the room is dressed in black and Lycra-clad, like highly trained ninja warriors, and the rest sport baggy cotton in various shades of sweat. But what draws us all together is our desire for some sort of transformative physical guidance. And at the age of 52, the oldest in the room I'm guessing, my desire is probably more than most.

I was a competitive gymnast as a child, winning a string of medals at the British Championships, including gold. It was not the typical Olympic style that many will be familiar with, involving beam and asymmetric bars and associated with the fame of Olga Korbut or Simone Biles, but a different kind of gymnastics called Sports Acrobatics which emerged in the UK in the 1970s, where girls or boys balance on top of each other and throw their partners through the air. Think circus but with pointy toes and fewer sequins and you are halfway there.

I had been plucked from obscurity in the after-school gym club by one of the teachers who also happened to be a coach at one of the city's top gymnastics clubs. No more roly-polys and playing at 'pirates' in the customary black plimsolls but rigorous, three-hour training sessions, four nights a week after school and frequent weekends when nearing competitions.

Back then, the only gyms were those dedicated to competitive sport or dingy basements where men could grunt their way through lifting weights. Knowledge of the body was pretty poor. Advancement was made through trial and error. When I was starting out around the age of nine, to achieve the splits meant lying on my back with one leg pointing to the ceiling as the hefty coach knelt across one knee and pushed the other down to reach my ear. He didn't stop – even when I cried. These days any physiotherapist (and I've had to visit quite a few of late) will tell you that stretch should be accompanied with strength and today's gymnasts work with different coloured rubber bands to put the muscles under tension. My coach was simply tearing me apart.

Luckily, an increased knowledge of biomechanics has now improved things to the point where even buying a pair of running shoes at a high street store can involve scientific assessment of the pronation of your gait. Gyms have become factory floors of machinery, each designed to target muscle groups and help align the body more effectively.

In Vienna though, there is no such scientific machinery – just bodies, and in the corner, wooden poles and a giant bag of tennis balls.

I sense our geckos have fallen short of expectations and we move onto another creature. This time we are monkeys balanced on our hands and swinging both legs together up and to the side in what looks like a half-hearted cartwheel. In recent years I've been a scorpion, a flamingo and, my personal favourite, a kangaroo. Imitating animal movements isn't new; almost every branch of yoga seems to have an *upward* or *downward dog* to unleash.

I am pretty good at being a monkey and think of relegating my kangaroo to second place. But it seems to be a greater challenge for others around the room where legs are flying in all directions. Upper bodies and lower limbs are disconnected and pitched against each other in never-ending combat. Bodies twist, crumple and collapse. I am surprised to see how difficult this relatively simple move is proving for so many, because on any sunny day at the beach, you will see children throwing themselves onto their hands, cartwheeling down the shore. They have no instructor, just an innate desire to tumble freely, experimenting with balance and having fun. These grown-ups in Vienna calculate and strategise, sometimes sketching out the physics in little notebooks before a hand is placed upon the floor.

Portal seems as mystified as me and calls us round for one of his many expositions. We all sit cross-legged before him – watching Jesus on the mount. Portal is not an imposing figure. No bulging muscles, no tower of strength. Before us stands a simple man in black T-shirt and white baggy cotton pants that stop halfway down his shins. He is surprisingly compact at only five foot five. No wonder we are all asked to sit.

He speaks with confidence and verve, animated by his passion. His words are precise and clipped by his slight Israeli accent. He tells us a little of his youth and how he had spent twenty years travelling the world, training and learning from a wide range of physically demanding perspectives – from boxers to runners, tennis players to fighters.

But he's bored of talking now and raises both his arms. 'OK,' he says, 'it's time to do the *worhk*!' He demonstrates some body waves, his face two inches from the wall. First the knees then the pelvis lean forward followed by his chest – one wave after the other in ceaseless undulation. 'Do fifty,' he says. We line up, shoulder to shoulder around the hall and begin to curl, gently loosening up the vertebrae. Next, we are put in pairs for an exercise to open up the thoracic spine – the bit that runs from the rib cage to the neck. Hands on the wall, arms stretched out at waist height, I begin the rounding and arching of my spine. My partner Lukas, an Austrian ex-professional football player, has the job of gently pressing his hands between my shoulder blades and counting.

We swap partners for the next activity and I turn to face a strapping man in his twenties with a red and black bandana round his head. I had seen these kinds of guys before standing outside the flagship stores of global clothing brands. Topless and ripped, they ride on sponsored open-top buses and embrace female shoppers in the street, posing for photos later put on Instagram. Their optimum goal of exercise is aesthetic, building a body in the perfect form. Being only five foot four, my eyes are at his chest

– a hairless chest which glistens. Between his pecs hangs his sweaty, cotton vest – dripping on the floor. This time we play the 'heat test' where one person stands, eyes closed, whilst the other touches the skin at random points around the body. 'Imagine,' says Portal, 'this touch is a red-hot poker thrust against the skin. Move away from it as quickly as you can. Let your instinct take over.' My muscleman waits, alert whilst in the dark, as I hesitate over which unsuspecting piece of flesh I should have a go at first. I prod and poke about a bit but despite his perfect muscle tone, his reactions are quite a disappointment. He may have the look of Tarzan swinging through the trees, but his instincts are clearly better matched with a modern concrete jungle.

It's time for another demonstration. Portal curls his fists and starts jabbing to the front and side. He explains that we use the body to put weight behind a punch in two ways: *ipsilateral,* where both the arm and foot move forward from the same side, whilst *contralateral* movements are more centred, using opposing arms and legs for stability. By switching between the two, we are engaging our bodies and our minds. In pairs, we are told to take turns shouting out *ipsi* or *contra* whilst our partner tries to respond with the correct foot and punching fist. There is a sense of renewed energy in the room as many of the men recognise the 'fighting talk' and leap to their feet. This is their domain, pretending to thump the crap out of someone in the comfort and security of their gym rather than the backstreet car park of their local bar. My heart sinks.

I find commercial gyms are designed to emulate the atmosphere of fight clubs – and the first punch is to the ear. Loud, thumping beats of techno, rap and electronica are pretty much the norm. Lyrics jab and uppercut, *bitch*, *whore* and *ass* – and much, much worse. On a rare day off, I decided to try a lunchtime class called *BOSU Ball*. It promised a range of exercises utilising half a large rubber ball mounted on a plastic base. There were only three of us in the class, so I was surprised to see the instructor adjusting his microphone and headset and placing a battery pack down his shorts. Within seconds, he had pressed play on some machine and the same tirade of misogyny and street slang for various drugs blared out to a monotonous beat. He had to shout to be heard but I had no idea what he was saying as the connection to my brain had been completely severed by the assault upon my senses.

Thump, thump, *bitch my ass,* 'and one and two' *and bitch my ass,* thump, thump, thump. It took three minutes for me to decide to leave – and the next twenty-five for me to realise that the only way to do it politely was to feign a heart attack and have a paramedic drag me out. If I had come to that conclusion earlier, I would have happily clenched my chest and dropped dramatically to the floor. But with only ten minutes or so left of the class it hardly seemed worth the bother.

There is no music in Portal's class just the breath of concentration and calls of *ipsi – contra, contra – ipsi*. My partner this time is a gangly man with glasses and wild, carefree hair. His bony arms thrust back and forth in an oversized and baggy T-shirt, reminding me of kittens trying to free themselves from a burlap sack. Despite his rather ragged appearance, he is surprisingly well co-ordinated. What he lacks in grace he makes up with precision. When it's my turn, I try to conjure up enthusiasm and respond quickly to his calls. *Ipsi* – right leg, right arm. *Contra* – right leg, left arm. 'Faster, faster!' shouts Portal as he inspects the room. As the pace quickens, there's a narrowing gap between my body and my mind and the movements seem to be happening on their own. Portal appears in front of me. 'Good,' he says, 'very good.' I am elated and just about suppress a thumping fist of victory.

SHANTELLE STEIN

As a former television journalist, Shantelle Stein loves exploring a new angle on a story. She has found this in a lesser-known chapter of Einstein's life when he was hidden by Commander Oliver Locker-Lampson owing to a Nazi bounty on his head.

shantelle.stein@gmail.com

The Road to Roughton
Excerpt from Chapter Three

Today we are going to the countryside. To a place where no one knows me. I am ecstatic in anticipation.
 —Albert Einstein, 10th Sept. 1933[1]

The Spirit of Ecstasy leapt into the air; chin and chest thrust forward, arms outstretched, clothes billowing behind like fairy wings. Had she not been restrained by the metal from which she was forged, it seemed at any given moment she might take off. This route up the A11 to Cromer was a familiar one, and as the official bonnet ornament of Rolls-Royce, she would guide the Phantom II safely to its destination. This recently released Phantom model was a refinement of the previous, boasting a new chassis, twenty-five horsepower and a synchromesh gearbox. Today, she would revel in this prowess.

Albert Einstein sat comfortably on the quilted leather upholstery. The prying eyes of nine dials assessed him from the varnished walnut dashboard. His reflection bounced back at him. He was tired. It had been two intense days of continuous travelling, with little reprieve. Now, he had a three-hour journey up to Cromer and then onto Roughton. Not that he, himself, would be driving. He could only ever be the passenger.

Commander Locker-Lampson, seated next to him, was at ease in the driver's seat, though his legs somewhat overshot the pedals. It was behind the wheel of a car that he felt most in control. His greatest exploits were dictated from this position. As early as 1909, at the age of twenty-nine, his Hotchkiss Landaulette 'burst into flames and became a ruin.' This proved yet another source of amusement to him, as did the time when he drove his Rolls-Royce into a river 'through overestimating the width of a bridge.' Damp and dishevelled and 'in a pair of trousers nearer his knees than his ankles, without a collar, with a red scarf and a pair of carpet slippers,' he still managed to address an enthusiastic political gathering just two hours after the accident.

---

1 Albert Einstein to Elsa Einstein, 8 September 1933, Albert Einstein Archives.

Locker-Lampson loved cars but he loved adventure more. The union of the two provided him with the experience he sought. In 1914, he used twenty thousand pounds of his own money and a blessing from Winston Churchill, then First Lord of the Admiralty, to form an armoured car division attached to the navy – the RNACD, squadron 15, comprising men local to Norfolk. The cars were specially fitted out by a coachbuilder, Duff Morgan and Vermont, in which Locker-Lampson was a silent business partner. They customised the interiors and bodies of all his armoured and personal transport. These vehicles fought on four fronts during the war, from Northern France and Belgium to the steppes and mountains of Russia and the plains of Romania. His unit formed the first expedition ever to leave British shores for duty with Russians in Russia.

On a map, the A11 wove from London up to Norfolk in a north westerly direction. At Norwich, Locker-Lampson took the A140 directly north to his home in Cromer and then later that same day drove to the final destination of Roughton. The latter still eluded the press, who were already stationed in Cromer. They knew nothing of a small wooden hut in a rented field. The journey covered little over one hundred and forty miles. It was generally uneventful in the direction of East Anglia, save for some minor delays caused by road widening work between Newmarket and Six Mile Bottom. With little under two million cars on the English roads, there was not much traffic, and the commander was able to move through the low-lying countryside with good speed. There was even time for them to stop for tea. The route offered a pleasant vista of flat countryside and quaint towns like Newmarket, where perfectly groomed, excitable horses walked in lines next to the road. Both men noticed the ravages of the recent drought as the land coughed chalky earth all around them. The Phantom would need to be cleaned again that evening. East Anglia was somewhat spared, though the land still looked scorched. This was no longer Constable country. There wasn't a hint of moisture; the horizon was clear and vast. More than half way through the journey they passed through Thetford Forest. The warm twenty-two degrees agitated the terpenes of the conifer trees causing them to release their fragrance while rows of Scots and Corsican pine helped prevent the sandy earth from blowing away. They were not near maturity, having only been planted within the last decade owing to timber shortages following the First World War.

Up in Leicester, more than two hours west of where the two men were driving, Lord Rutherford, the Australian physicist, was giving a speech. It was exactly twenty-six years since Lord Kelvin, an Irish physicist, stood in the same place declaring that the atom was indestructible and could never be split. Lord Rutherford proudly refuted this claim today, saying the atom could in fact be split into more than eighty constituent parts. There was a disclaimer though:

'The energy produced by the breaking down of the atom is a very poor kind of thing. Anyone who expects a source of power from transformation of these atoms is talking moonshine. We hope in the next few years to get some idea of what these atoms are, how they are made, and the way they are worked.'

Einstein was in agreement. To him the notion of creating energy from atoms was tantamount to 'shooting birds in the dark.' He saw no practical way to release it. Back in London though, his friend and colleague, Leo Szilar, had just experienced an epiphany. What if neutrons could be harnessed, instead of alpha particles, to do the job of unleashing this energy and creating a nuclear chain reaction? This insight would help guide scientific thought, ultimately resulting in the atomic bomb.

It was shortly after five pm when the Rolls-Royce pulled up outside Newhaven Court on Norwich Road in Cromer. The seaside town was a popular retreat for many and was in the middle of its annual summer carnival. The fair's organiser, Edgar Ackerman, was still counting the total raised from its recent successful August event. In two days, he would announce that the £880 collected would be donated to the Cromer and District Hospital. Locker-Lampson was involved with the annual occasion, bringing dignitaries like the King and Queen of Greece to raise the profile of these local festivities. Today, many in the town knew the Commander was to receive a visitor of great import, though a celebrity sighting at the family home was not a novelty. Every summer, when the Commander moved from London up to his Norfolk retreat, the house became a menagerie of sorts, teeming with colourful characters like Ernest Shackleton, Oscar Wilde and Churchill. Newhaven Court, now the Royal Cromer Hotel, had been in the family since 1883, purchased by Sir Curtis Lampson, the first American to be bestowed an English title, and the man responsible for laying the initial transatlantic cable. The estate was later granted to his daughter, Jane, on condition that she kept the family name. A grateful son-in-law, Frederick Locker, took the name and the property willingly. Newhaven Court had unrestricted views of the local area and for that privilege it suffered the wrath of the elements. According to Frederick, 'it faces the sea on a windswept hill – in winter it's empty – in summer it's chill. Indeed it is one of the earth's wildest spots as we know from the smashing of the chimney pots. In August I ask for an extra quilt, this is the house that Jane built.'

Einstein was given a tour of the large Arts and Crafts building. It was a 'pavilion of charm' according to its owner. The fully-lit, covered tennis court that hosted professional players, always found its way into conversations (Locker-Lampson's name-dropping was as legendary as the people who frequented the property). His musings inevitably included his friendship with Lord Balfour.

'I played Arthur Balfour three sets of stiff tennis on his 77th birthday and he wrote that evening a critique on metaphysics which highbrows called not merely masterly in its grasp but daring in its youthful challenge to tradition. He never seemed to age. Can it really be true that we shall never again watch that slim, casual form in its grey flannels and brown shoes executing deadly cut shots with a racket from the baseline?'

Newhaven's interiors offered a catalogue of delights. All the objets d'art demonstrated the family's wildly eclectic tastes. Some were indeed treasures, like a pen-and-ink Van Dyck head and one of Holbein's pencil portraits. These stared out over coins, pipes, patch-boxes and a China owl of 'famed prestige' (though later, Frederick was to admit he had been swindled again) and a double-handled wine jar, purportedly once the property of William Shakespeare, despite the rumour that Tennyson (a frequent visitor at Newhaven) 'shook the room with Homeric laughter' at Frederick's exhibition of the supposed artefact. The Locker-Lampsons were evidently as much collectors of people as they were of things.

At half past six, Einstein was spotted by an *Eastern Daily Press* journalist walking in the gardens of Newhaven. The estate was large and a walk promised a good dose of fresh sea air from the North Sea. The two men gathered once more by the Rolls-Royce. Einstein's hair looked more dishevelled that usual, having battled with the elements, while the commander's remained unmoved in its usual Brylcreem sweep. A group from the media mulled about, hoping to glean something about this visit. There had been rumours. The professor, while still reticent, seemed more relaxed already, and permitted a brief interaction.

'The Nazi threat had an indirect influence on the professor's movements this weekend.' Locker-Lampson began by dismissing the threat on the professor's life. 'The report about a price being set upon his head is incredible. It has to be explored however. And the matter will be gone into.'

'I just want peace,' Einstein declared, 'and could I have found a more peaceful retreat than here in England? At Le Coq I was always guarded. It was a terrible strain and a great responsibility to be put on the Belgian police. It interfered with my work. My friend has invited me here, and I hope to stay in England for a month. No one will know where I am until October. I can live quietly, working out my mathematical problems.'

There was a distinct fondness developing between the two men.

'The professor is modest. He is engaged on a new mathematical theory.'

Albert Einstein smiled. He made no comment on what the theory was. Instead, he changed the subject.

'I was not responsible for the Brown Book. I was on the committee which authorised the publication of the book, but I did not write anything in it although I agreed with its content.'

This statement was not entirely in line with what the commander had suggested he might say and doubtless he would have some explaining to do to Professor Yahuda. The two men had agreed that Einstein needed to create absolute distance from the matter, and such words were still ambiguous, inviting speculation from not only the press but the Nazis as well. They were listening, and very possibly looking out for him. Such was the threat.

They had little over an hour before the sun was due to set. As they drove off in the direction of Roughton, thousands of swallows draped the telephone wires like a long sapphire necklace. They bobbed rhythmically as they prepared for their imminent departure across the channel. It may not have felt like it, given the unseasonable heat, but that summer's days were numbered.

JILL VAUGHAN

Jill Vaughan studied Physical Geography and Soil Science. She writes about the Wiltshire landscape where she and generations of her family grew up, and the people who lived and worked there. Inspired by her father's tales, she is fascinated by how walking links landscape, stories and memories.

jillvaughan56@gmail.com

The Place of Springs
This is an abridged first chapter from a book based around my father's stories and my memories.

Devizes is a market town in Wiltshire and Potterne a large village two miles south-southwest of it; I was born in the former and my father in the latter. I only lived in Devizes from the ages of five to eighteen, but the area within an hour's walk from my birthplace is my heartland. When I walk in north Cambridgeshire, where I live now, the contrast between the flat, rectilinear, agri-industrial fenland and the countryside where I grew up couldn't be starker. The word that best describes the feeling engendered by walking the fens is *hiraeth*, a Welsh word for a longing, yearning nostalgia. I want to explore why I connect so strongly with the landscape around Devizes. To what extent is it due to associations with people and a happy childhood and how much to the intrinsic qualities of the landscape?

It is ironic that what enhances my understanding and appreciation of the area is what took me away from it in the first place. I studied geography at London University, and it was moving to the capital that first made me acutely aware of how important my homeland really was to me.

An inspirational schoolteacher first introduced me to the geology of the surrounding area. This was an epiphany for me. Until then, everything we had been taught was about places I'd never been. The Vale of Pewsey is a funnel-shaped area of low-lying ground running eastwards from the heart of Wiltshire between the opposing escarpments of the Marlborough Downs and Salisbury Plain. Devizes and Potterne are situated on two of the three promontories of land guarding its western approaches.

The route I am going to describe traverses four rock types: Lower Chalk, Upper Greensand, Gault and the Portland Beds which mark the transition to the older Jurassic rocks. The term 'chalk and cheese' is used in Wiltshire to describe how sheep were kept on the downs and dairy cows in the clay vales. A more local phrase is 'chalk and church', because in the elongated parishes on the chalk, villages cluster around the church at the foot of the escarpment. In the cheese country, the villages are less compact, and the farms spread over the pastures at intervals of double the walking distance of a cow, so there was more opportunity for nonconformist chapels.

Because the pervious Upper Greensand lies on top of impervious Gault clay, there are numerous springs. In his memoir of Potterne, Thomas Smith lists six: Pitchers & Pans, Sugar Well, Horse Well, Wick Well, Grub's Shrub (haunted) and Bottomless Well. 'The Place of Springs' was used by the former Potterne primary school on its badge.

Our walk begins at the Southgate Inn. It wasn't one of my watering holes, but my parents used to drink there in their courting days. If Devizes were a Monopoly board, we'd have the Park Lane and Mayfair squares on our left – one side road still has a gate across it to prevent the hoi polloi from using it as a rat run.

John Palmer in full regalia – the 'WP' on his apron stands for 'Worthy Primo'.

My great-grandfather John Palmer used to sweep the chimneys of many of the big houses, cycling with rods tied to the crossbar of his bike, and his printed business cards in his pocket. At the end of his working life (in his seventies), he was cycling in thick fog along this same road towards Potterne. Probably missing a turning, he hit the bank with considerable force. He was never the same afterwards. Despite his minimal formal education, he was an active member of the Wesleyan Chapel and later rented his own pew in the Methodist Church in Devizes; his daughter lived long enough to see me married there. My father remembers him heading off to chapel in his Sunday best three-piece suit, complete with hat (not a cap) and furled umbrella. He was also Worthy Primo of the Royal Antediluvian Order of Buffaloes, a fraternal charitable organisation.

The road then descends through a deep, shady cutting, with trees on both sides. Stanley Smith-Douse, a plasterer by trade and often plastered himself, nearly came to grief here. He and his mates used to frequent The Bell in Potterne, known as 'The Scrumpy House'. The cider gang fell out with the landlord and decamped to the Southgate Inn where we began our walk. Here they were famous for 'The Dance of the Dying Swan'. Suitably lubricated, they would climb onto the cast-iron tables with round wooden tops. They would then fall off, without any attempt to lessen the impact. On his way home from one of these sessions, Stanley reached the bottom of the hill where he overbalanced and fell through the hedge. He was unable to climb back up the bank, so spent the night where he lay. 'When I woke up, I were covered with 'oar vrost,' he told my dad.

A quarter of a mile up the road is Sandfield Farm where I used to keep my pony. Riding out from this farm I learned all the tracks and byways that my grandmother's family had used. I also became a farm labourer – I had to earn the money for the ton of hay it took to feed my pony through the winter, the field rent, shoeing and other expenses.

A bit further on we pass the former Bell Inn, home of the cider gang before they were banned. The road goes through another cutting overlooked by the beautiful thirteenth-century Church of St Mary on the edge of the Greensand scarp that the road skirts round. During restorations in 1872, a tenth-century Saxon font was found under the floor. The Latin inscription from St Jerome around its rim is apt for the 'Place of Springs':

Like as the hart desireth the water-brooks, so longeth my soul after Thee, O God.

Though John Palmer was a nonconformist, his daughter Lois married William Vaughan in St Mary's on 23 April 1927. Born before their first wedding anniversary, my father was christened here at the same time as Lois's brother's first child, Albert (pronounced 'Olburt' by the family), who was only two days old. Thomas Smith recounts, 'It was customary to fetch water from Pitchers & Pans for christening purposes. This was quite a common custom, especially amongst the Wesleyans.' No doubt the practice had died out before my father was christened, but perhaps one of his Palmer forbears was baptised with spring water?

It is said that men from Potterne excel at three things: working, drinking and fighting. John Palmer was certainly a hard worker, and always had a bob or two in his pocket. As well as his chimney-sweeping business, he worked allotments, growing enough carrots and parsnips to pay the rent on his cottage.

Out of six pubs that existed in 1900, and three when I was a girl, only one remains – The George & Dragon, home of the Potterne Mummers. Despite being a 'chapel ranter', John Palmer had his own quart pot at the George. The oldest part of the pub is of timber-framed cruck construction and may be fifteenth century. The area in front is known as 'The Bash' where the stocks once stood. There are two flights of stairs on the outside leading down from the front door. Fights were held here with each man trying to knock the other down the opposite steps. Natives of Potterne are known as 'Lambs' or 'Baas' as they had a reputation for hooliganism before Superintendent Wolfe of the Wiltshire Constabulary was involved in putting down a riot in 1857.

Opposite the pub is Coxhill Lane where Dad first saw the light of day, cradled under the cruck truss in 'Cosy Cot', a cottage as old as the George. However, our route takes us on along the main road through another deep cutting dug through the Greensand by French prisoners during the Napoleonic wars. Further along is Eastwell House, home of the Hunt-Grubbes. There is a stone cottage loaf on the gate posts, a sign in more generous times that passing hungry travellers would be fed if they called at the kitchen. Whether this custom was kept when my great-grandmother was cook there, I don't know.

We are now at the far end of the village known as Potterne Wick. A quiet lane forks to the left and wanders off towards Urchfont (pronounced 'Ushunt' by the locals). John Palmer and his wife Elizabeth lived here in their early married life. She was pregnant with my gran at the same time as the lady of Eastwell House, who also gave birth to a daughter whom she named Lois; my gran was named after her. When my daughter was born (the first of her great-granddaughters), I christened her Lois. 'What did you want to call her that for?' said Gran, but I hope she was secretly pleased.

Gran's older brother Jack was a farmworker on the Hunt-Grubbes' farm at Cadley, about fifteen minutes' walk across the fields. I remember Uncle Jack – an epic snorer with huge hands dominated by Mabel, a wife half his size. Believing that the farmer didn't give the horses enough feed for the work they were doing, he used to lift a slate from the roof of the locked granary and steal extra rations for them. His horses were called Drummer and Prince and my dad used to ride on their broad backs when he stayed at Cadley, by way of a holiday. The other ploughman was Jinnet, brother of the cider drinker who fell through the hedge.

Great Uncle Jack, with Drummer and Prince. Note the elm trees in the hedge.

However, we will take a sharp left up Saddleback Lane which takes us past Sugarwell and joins up with Coxhill Lane. This sunken track, layered with leaf mould, hugs the north side of Potterne Woods (an ancient and semi-natural woodland). From there a footpath leads northwest to the summit of the chalk outlier called One Tree Hill and though lower than the downs, its distinctive shape made it a landmark for miles around. It used to have a single huge elm at its summit, said to have been planted by General Hunt-Grubbe to commemorate the Battle of Waterloo. During my teens, Dutch elm disease wiped out the 'Wiltshire Weed'. Uncle Harry (the Sandfield farmer) had the tree inoculated, but it succumbed to the disease. An oak was planted to replace it.

In 2017 I visited Potterne with my father, eighty-nine years to the day since he was baptised at St Mary's. After ploughman's and pints in The George & Dragon we explored our old haunts. The topography dictated that the new estates that have kept the village alive were built away from the main road, so the High Street looks much the same as it did when John Palmer lived there. Coxhill Lane was even more idyllic than I remembered, seen through eyes sensitised by thirty-three years in the fens. The banks were full of ferns and spring flowers, between tree roots exploring every joint in the greensand.

As we stood on One Tree Hill taking in the hazy view south-westwards, it was a perfect spring day, with larks singing in a cloudless, cornflower-blue sky. Strangely, Potterne is almost invisible from up here, hidden in hollow ways. The older buildings blend into the landscape, being made of local materials: Potterne Stone, timber crucks and red bricks handmade from the Gault. Everything belongs, nothing is superimposed. So, I think my feeling of being uprooted is as much to do with the landscape as being one hundred and seventy miles away from my extended family and friends, most of whom stayed near home or moved back. Straight lines for waterways and roads and everything at one height (sea level or below) make me uneasy. The tales linked to places here belong to others. Fenlanders can feel claustrophobic when removed from their uninterrupted horizons, but I long to be up on the chalk looking down at a green vale or wondering what's over the hill or round the next bend.

Thomas Smith, Potterne 1850–1900 (unpublished, 1983).
P M Slocombe, 'The George & Dragon Inn, Potterne,' *Wiltshire Archaeological and Natural History Magazine* 77 (1983): 87–92.
Paul Robinson, 'Royal Justice and Folk Justice: Conflict Arising over a Skimmington in Potterne in 1857,' *Wiltshire Archaeological and Natural History Magazine* 83 (1990): 147–54.
N B Chapman and P M Slocombe, 'A Domestic Cruck Building at Potterne,' *Wiltshire Archaeological and Natural History Magazine* 76 (1982): 105–8.

QINGHUA ZHU

Qinghua Zhu received her MA from the Communication University of China in 2013, majoring in Chinese Literature. She worked for seven years as a journalist at Yunnan TV in the southwest of China. In 2020 she was selected as a Chevening scholar and began studying creative non-fiction writing at UEA.

qinghua.zhu87@outlook.com

Tea or Coffee?

When I walked into Square Street at the centre of Shaxi, I immediately felt like I was in ancient times. More than two hundred stones lay on the ground, leftover from the Qing dynasty. The sunlight was filtering through the leaves of acacia trees which touched the cornice of the ancient theatre, and in the dappled light and shadow, you could still see its original patterns, which seem to be a distant murmur of ancient history. On the left and right of the stage, there were rows of two-storey Chinese traditional timber-framed houses, each with a wooden counter outside the window on the ground floor.

Then I saw Yang, about forty years old, a farmer from another neighbouring village, who was busy with farm work before working at the Sophora Tree Café. I ordered a cup of mocha.

Coffee is not as popular as tea in China's vast rural areas. I was curious about why the café would hire a middle-aged Bai woman as a waitress.

'Yang, do you like coffee and which one do you prefer?' I asked.

'I had never seen coffee before, never had a cup of coffee, and I only learned to make coffee when I came here to work,' she replied.

Yang and I talked in Mandarin. Her accent was a little heavy, yet we are both Bai, one of China's fifty-five ethnic minorities, and we have our own language. She chose not to speak it because here her customers are also Mandarin-speaking people from other provinces, or simply foreigners. Her boss is from Shenzhen, a large southern city across the sea from Hong Kong, which has the most dynamic economy.

Shenzhen and Shaxi met here.

Other shops in the square sell traditional handicrafts, ethnic clothing and, in the afternoons, you can often find elderly Bai women wearing dark-blue Bai double-breasted blouses and aprons, their hair pulled back in a bun and tied up with an equally dark-blue headscarf. They sit on wooden steps and embroider, stitch by stitch, in the sunshine, flicking a needle and thread up and down quickly in their right hands, without a hint of modernity – it is an image that Western photographers can't get enough of.

There is an international youth hostel on the edge of the square, owned by a Taiwanese woman, who has signed a ten-year lease at a fairly low price. She fell in love with Shaxi at first sight. In the early morning, a layer of mist hangs over the river, the air is thin and crisp, filled with hazy sunshine and frost. Patches of rice ears droop in the sunshine and Bai women's baskets are filled with fresh vegetables ready to be sold at the market.

Taiwan and Shaxi also met here.

Before the arrival of the people of Shenzhen and Taiwan, the place was in a state of decay and desolation. The wooden houses were crooked and crumbling, the tiles on the roofs were covered with thick weeds, there were few footsteps on the cobbles, and everything was fading like the couplets on the doorways.

However, the arrival of a Swiss man changed all that.

Dr Jacques, from Switzerland, is the discoverer of Shaxi.

In 2000, Dr Jacques, a Swiss cultural heritage conservation expert, came to Dali Prefecture by chance and discovered Shaxi from the viewing pavilion of Shibao Mountain. Small in scale and concentrated in ancient architecture, it looks like a place that can replicate the Swiss model of ancient architecture restoration. Back in Switzerland, Dr Jacques submitted Shaxi to the World Monuments Fund (WMF).

In October 2001, WMF announced in New York that Shaxi in Yunnan, China, was to be added to the World Monuments Watch List of 100 Most Endangered Sites in 2001 with commentary that referenced Shaxi's former glory.

The Shaxi Market Area in China's Yunnan Province is the most complete surviving example of a trading centre along the historic Tea and Horse Caravan Trail, which linked Tibet with Southeast Asia between the fourteenth and nineteenth centuries.

Switzerland and Shaxi met here.

The Ancient Tea and Horse Caravan Trail was a Chinese commercial network comparable to the Silk Road. For thousands of years, it was a trade route between the Han and Tibetan peoples that crossed the Qinghai-Tibet Plateau and mainland China. It was the highest and most treacherous ancient route known in the world.

Once upon a time, horse gangs followed this rugged and bumpy road, carrying tea, salt, cloth and other necessities for the Tibetan lands, and then exchanging them for horses, cattle, sheep and furs, which is how the Tea and Horse Caravan Trail got its name.

Shaxi flourished for a time with merchants.

After the middle of the last century, transportation was upgraded, cars took the place of horses, and the Tea and Horse Caravan Trail declined.

The fate of the town is tied up with the history of iterations of transport. The pulse of the car cut through the time and the daily life of the town. The bustling scene portrayed in *Caravans with Ring* (1954)[1] is history, and the noisy square returned to tranquillity. This tranquillity was maintained for fifty years.

Then in 2003, the Swiss restoration team brought in 14 million yuan (1.6 million pounds) in international funds. This transnational generosity woke up the sleepy town of Shaxi. At the same time as the restoration work was being prepared, Chinese architect Huang was about to graduate from the Swiss Federal Institute of Technology. He joined the preparatory team as the Swiss director of the Shaxi Restoration Project.

I met Huang in the square to discuss his work. He is thin, light on his feet, with clear eyes and a gentle voice: the intellectual image of a modest gentleman.

'Do you remember how it was when you first came to Shaxi?' I asked.

'Shaxi was like an old thing abandoned in a yard, and suddenly a passer-by thought it was good and said he'd like to fix it up. The owner of the thing thought it didn't matter, you could fix it if you wanted to.'

The stones beneath our feet have been here for hundreds of years. These old stones, round and pitted, are anachronistic in the face of modern transport. The local authorities had wanted to dig them up and replace them with new stones to make a smooth, wide road, of a standard passable for trucks, so that construction could be carried out more quickly. Huang had insisted that the original stones would remain where they were when they were repaired. They even stopped work twice due to a difference of opinion.

The controversy ended with Huang's solution winning, as the Swiss Restoration Fund was not in the hands of the government after all. At the time, the Chinese government was, Huang says, 'rather hazy about the whole restoration project' and 'didn't take the remote town very seriously. The attitude of the government was that the money was yours anyway, so do what you like!'

In the end, the square, which is over sixty metres long from north to south and twenty metres wide from east to west, was left with the old stones intact. The restoration team numbered each stone and put them back in place again. To gaze upon them is to look back on history.

---

1 *Caravans with Ring*, 1954. [film] Directed by Weiyi Wang. China: Shanghai Film Studios.

Huang and I walk down the old flagstone street. The streams on either side of the road flow in a trickling, silent current; the early morning sun gently caresses every inch of the stone; the water splashes, reflecting the blue sky high above us.

'I'm curious. Do the locals understand that you're here to fix a shabby house like this?' I ask, pointing to one such building in desperate need of attention.

'It's not even really understood, it's just why we spend so much effort and so much money on trivial things. People will think why bother pushing so hard, it's too common for them to have a house like this.'

The project team spent the next six months restoring all of Shaxi's public buildings, ancient theatres and squares with archaeological rigour and high quality, then in 2005, the Shaxi Restoration Project won the UNESCO Asia-Pacific Heritage Conservation Award.

More and more voices say that Shaxi has become noisier, that original life is becoming less and less authentic, and that locals are powerless to fight back against foreign capital.

Huang and I strolled around the square and went into the home of local villager Yin, who had returned to his old house on the edge of the square after a successful restoration, to start a handicraft business. He abandoned this old wooden structure and built a modern, concrete two-storey house outside the village many years ago. 'It's more respectable to live in a concrete house, like city people,' he said.

For most villagers, building a house is not an exacting drawing of plans, it is more like a social process in which social identity symbols are a more important matter. The owners of the concrete houses are always richer than the owners of wooden ones. What the villagers need more than aesthetic distinctions is social identity.

'Hello, Huang Xiansheng!' From a distance, the sound of a horse's bell preceded the rich male voice.

We met Zhao, in his sixties, dressed in full Bai costume. Zhao wraps his head in a white headdress, which accentuates his dark complexion from long exposure to the ultraviolet rays of the plateau. He wears a white double-breasted coat, with a dark-blue waistcoat over it, and carries a small, exquisitely embroidered purse. He was leading his horse, on which sits a stylishly dressed young woman, wearing heavy make-up and high heels, clearly unfit to walk on these ancient stones.

The hustle and bustle of tourists bring in the money. Some things that are commonplace to locals have become cash cows. Zhao's ancestors have been raising horses for generations. He now put bells on his horses and started a business for tourists, and he was the first in the village to start a horse-riding business. For sixty yuan (seven pounds), you can ride five km on Zhao's horse.

Some other culture shocks have emerged. Once upon a time, the central hall in an old house was a place of worship for the ancestors, a sacred place that could not be converted into a bathroom or guest room at will. 'It doesn't exist anymore: I rent it to you and don't care what you want to do.' Zhao seems no longer to have an attachment to his ancestors.

The old houses are not so much a cultural heritage in their eyes as a tool for a comfortable life. For them, there is nothing more tangible than a better life. Simplicity and insecurity, poverty and pride, it's all in their faces.

From where we sit, looking through the open wooden window frame, Yang sits at the coffee table, distracted by the setting sun that splits her face in half, one side light, the other dark.

She had never had coffee before, and now she makes coffee for foreign tourists, but still can't tell the difference between a cappuccino and a caramel macchiato.

She is often ridiculed for her simplicity. When the owner of another café saw that I had bought a mocha from Yang, he asked me, 'someone who has worked all her life in agriculture and does not know how to taste coffee; is the coffee she sells drinkable?'

'It doesn't matter. I don't know how to taste coffee, anyway.' I replied.

ACKNOWLEDGEMENTS

This anthology contains the work written by the 2021 cohort of UEA's MA in Creative Writing: Biography and Creative Non-Fiction. We are very grateful for the support of the UEA School of Literature and Egg Box Publishing, part of UEA Publishing Project, Ltd., without whom this anthology would not have been published.

We would like to thank our course director, Helen Smith, for her support and the writing of the introduction for this anthology. Thanks also to our course tutors Kathryn Hughes and Ian Thomson whose insights were greatly appreciated.

We are extremely grateful to our guest author, Elisa Segrave, for her class discussion and the writing of the foreword for this anthology. Thanks also for the class contributions from Sharon Tolaini-Sage and Victor Sage.

Huge thanks to Shannon Clinton-Copeland, Nathan Hamilton, Emily Benton and Sarah Gooderson at the UEA Publishing Project for their help in managing, designing and proofreading this anthology. Thanks also to our hard-working Non-Fiction editors Gordon Clark, Frances Lord, Constance Harris and Jannita Smith.

With grateful thanks to all the donors who contribute to the scholarships that support our writers, including: Chevening Scholarship, Marshall Scholarship and the International Excellence Scholarship.

Lastly, of course, huge gratitude to all our fellow students whose friendship, patience and kindness have been invaluable – especially in this 'lockdown' year.

UEA MA Creative Writing Anthologies: Non-Fiction

First published by Egg Box Publishing, 2021
Part of the UEA Publishing Project Ltd.

International © retained by individual authors

This book is sold subject to the condition that it shall not, by way of trade or otherwise, be lent, resold, hired out, stored in a retrieval system, or otherwise circulated without the publisher's prior consent in any form of binding or cover other than that in which it is published and without a similar condition including this condition being imposed on the subsequent purchaser.

A CIP record for this book is available from the British Library
Printed and bound in the UK by Imprint Digital

Designed by Emily Benton Book Design
emilybentonbookdesign.co.uk

Proofread by Sarah Gooderson

Distributed by NBN International
10 Thornbury Road
Plymouth
PL6 7PP
+44 (0)1752 202 301
e.cservs@nbninternational.com

ISBN 978-1-913861-28-5